W9-BDU-133

Editor
Elin Cook, M.S. Ed.

Editorial Project Manager
Elizabeth Morris, Ph.D.

Editor in Chief
Sharon Coan, M.S. Ed.

Creative Director
Elayne Roberts

Imaging
Alfred Lau

Production Manager
Phil Garcia

Acknowledgments:
PowerPoint software is 1983–2000
Microsoft Corporation. All Rights
Reserved. PowerPoint is a registered
Trademark of Microsoft Corporation.

Publishers:
Rachelle Cracchiolo, M.S. Ed.
Mary Dupuy Smith, M.S. Ed.

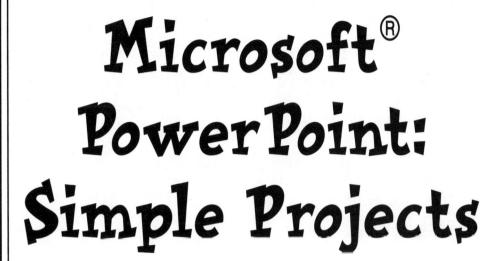

Microsoft® PowerPoint: Simple Projects

Intermediate

Author:

Corinne Burton

Teacher Created Materials, Inc.
6421 Industry Way
Westminster, CA 92683
www.teachercreated.com
ISBN-1-57690-441-0
©2000 Teacher Created Materials, Inc.
Made in U.S.A.

Table of Contents

Introduction

Simple Projects for PowerPoint is your guidebook to exciting curriculum-centered computer activities. The projects presented in this book use the resources of the computer to augment your curriculum. The activities are based on content in the five major curriculum areas: language arts, social studies, science, math, and art. Each lesson has been assigned a subject area, but do not let that stop you from integrating the lessons into other areas of your curriculum. Use the Language Arts Postcards lesson to teach geography. Teach writing skills within the context of any of the lessons in social studies, language arts, science topics, or art. Transfer the ideas for taking a survey from "Our Favorite Cookies" to a science lesson in which students need to tabulate data. These lessons are flexible enough to use again and again.

Some of you may prefer the format of a cookbook with easy-to-follow instructions listed out step-by-step. This is available in each lesson to use as a demonstration guide or to duplicate and hand out to your students. Once your students have mastered the skills necessary for each activity, the step-by-step instructions will guide them along, leaving you free to work with other students on different activities.

Now that the future is here and computer technology is a part of your classroom, we hope that *Simple Projects for PowerPoint* helps you make a smooth transition as you integrate technology into your curriculum. Allow the computer to work for you, and the resulting products will be fabulous.

Please note that this book was written from the perspective of *PowerPoint 97 for Windows*. If you have another version of the software, you will still be able to use these lessons to create flashy presentations. However, you may need to modify a step or two depending on the version of *Microsoft PowerPoint* that you own.

Understanding the Instructions

As you read through this book, there will be times you are given specific instructions to follow. You might have to select an item from the menu bar. You might have to type in a specific word or name, or you might need to choose a specific button by clicking on the mouse. Use this guide for following the directions that are given to you.

Instruction	What To Do
BOLD CAPITALS	Select this pulldown menu from the Menu Bar.
Bold Italics	Make this selection from the pulldown menu.
Bold	Choose this button, tool, or key.
(filename)	Type this word or sentence, or this is the name of a file.

Using This Book

About the CD-ROM

Turn to the back of this book and you will find a CD-ROM. It contains resource files for each of the projects in this book. This book is intended for readers who have a version of *PowerPoint* residing on their computer. The CD-ROM does not contain the software application itself. You will be able to read the files on the CD-ROM if you are using *PowerPoint 97* for Windows or *Power Point 98* for Macintosh.

Nearly every project in *PowerPoint Simple Projects* has associated CD-ROM files. The template files associated with the projects are already created for you. Template files are meant for you to open and immediately save under another name somewhere on your desktop, hard drive, or floppy diskette. (Since the CD-ROM is *read-only*, you cannot save the changes you make to any file on the CD-ROM.) That way the original template file is always intact and ready for you to use again and again. So, if you open a template file, before entering any text or data, click on the **FILE** menu and select *Save As*. Navigate to where you want to save your file, rename it, and then click on the **Save** button. Then you can begin entering text and data, knowing that the original file is still intact. That's all there is to using a template file!

Feel free to create a *PowerPoint Simple Projects* folder on your desktop or hard drive and download all the files from the CD-ROM into it for your convenience. Here's an organizational tip: Create a **My PowerPoint Presentations** folder within that folder to keep the files you complete as you work through the book. Don't you just love being organized?

CD-ROM File Names
Templates (Templates folder)

Page	Activity	Description	Macintosh File Name	Windows File Name
19	Postcards	Student Template	Postcard	Postcard.ppt
23	Story Sequencing	Student Template	Story	Story.ppt
26	Sell the Book	Student Template	Book	Book.ppt
30	Electronic Yearbook	Teacher Template	Yearbook	Yearbook.ppt
39	National Symbols	Student Template	National	National.ppt
42	Native Americans	Student Template	Native	Native.ppt
54	The American Government	Student Template	Govern	Govern.ppt
58	Touring the Solar System	Student Template	Solar	Solar.ppt
62	Nutrition	Student Template	Pyramid	Pyramid.ppt
68	Discovering Matter	Student Template	Matter	Matter.ppt
72	Animal Report	Student Template	Animal	Animal.ppt
78	Our Favorite Cookies	Student Template	Cookies	Cookies.ppt
81	Geometric Shapes	Student Template	Shapes	Shapes.ppt
84	Math with Candies	Student Template	Math	Math.ppt

Examples (Examples folder)

Page	Activity	Description	Macintosh File Name	Windows File Name
50	Family Tree	Example	Family	Family.ppt
81	Geometric Shapes	Example	Circle	Circle.ppt
84	Math with Candies	Example	Candies	Candies.ppt

Picture Files (Pictures folder)

For Use with the Touring the Solar System Activity

Picture	File Name
Solar System	solarsys.gif
Small Sun	smallsun.gif
Big Sun	bigsun.jpg

Getting Started

PowerPoint is an exciting and fun program that provides hundreds of opportunities for you and your students. This program provides teachers with a way to create personal teacher presentations for students or for staff development and for student-generated presentations. This book will focus on simple projects that your students can complete on the computer. If you're not as familiar as you'd like to be with the features and capabilities of *PowerPoint*, check out *PowerPoint for Terrified Teachers* (TCM2440).

This book contains activities from all the major subject areas such as language arts, mathematics, science, social studies, and fine arts. Your students will learn how to take data, turn it into a chart and present it on a slide in the Our Favorite Cookies and Math with Candies activities. They will create slide show reports that provide textual and photographic information on people, places, and historic sites in the My Famous Artist, Native American Report, and Postcards activities. Students will become familiar with how to create their own templates for presentation in such activities as All About Me and My Famous Artist. They will also learn to use *PowerPoint's* AutoLayout templates with graphics, text, and organizational charts in Family Tree and Discovering Matter.

Once these presentations have been created, they can be used in a variety of ways. Students can demonstrate their presentation to other students in the classroom or in the school. Presentations can be saved and used as a learning tool as students explore their peers' reports during computer and free time. The presentations can be saved as HTML files and posted on a school or classroom Web site for parents, teachers, and students to access throughout the world. Providing your students with the opportunity to learn and experiment with *PowerPoint* will give them a head start on the skills necessary in today's working society!

Getting Started *(cont.)*

Let's get started. Open the *PowerPoint* program and the New Presentation dialog box appears.

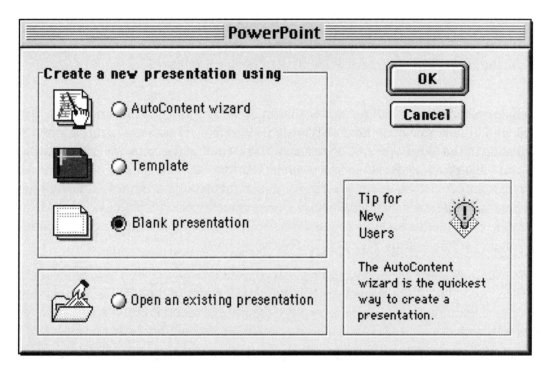

You have four options at this point. The first one is to select the **AutoContent Wizard**. Check this out when you have a couple of minutes. It provides a good overview of *PowerPoint* as well as ways to utilize the program in your everyday life. This is a great tool to become familiar with so you can explain to students and parents how important learning a presentation slide show program is in the "real world." It will also give you some ideas on how you can utilize the program in your teaching.

Your second option is to select the **Template**. This option provides you with a variety of formats you can select for a consistent look throughout your presentation. You and your students will not be using these standard format templates for any of the projects in this book, but they are useful when you are creating any *PowerPoint* presentations from scratch.

Your third option is the **Blank Presentation**. You will be using this option throughout the *Simple Projects* book. This provides you with a slide which has no standard format. From there, you are able to add text boxes, graphic boxes, organizational charts, or chart boxes. You will be utilizing many of these elements throughout the book.

Your final option on the opening screen is **Opening an Existing Presentation**. You will be using this option throughout the book. Many of the activities in this book include templates for the students to use. These templates are located on a CD in the back of the book. To access them, you or your students will need to insert the CD into your computer's CD-ROM player, select **Opening an Existing Presentation**, and then choose the appropriate template.

PowerPoint Tips and Tricks

Viewing Your Presentation

PowerPoint provides multiple ways to view your slide show presentation. You can access these options either through a toolbar on your screen or by pulling down the **VIEW** menu.

▢ Slide View

With this option, your slide show automatically pops up when you open a new presentation or open an existing presentation from the CD. While you are in **Slide View**, you can create, edit, and change your slides at any time. If you are in another view (such as **Outline View**) and want to return to **Slide View**, pull down the **VIEW** menu and select *Slide*. You can also click on the **Slide View** icon on the screen.

▤ Outline View

This view presents the text in an outline format. It is a useful tool for students who are going to be presenting their slide show to the class. It can serve as a reminder of the material they are presenting. To access this option, click on the **Outline View** icon or pull down the **VIEW** menu and select *Outline*.

▦ Slide Sorter View

Once a slide show is complete, you can click on the **Slide Sorter View** and view your slides all at once. You can click and drag the slides around to rearrange the order of your slide show presentation. To access this option:

- Click on the **Slide Sorter View** icon or pull down the **VIEW** menu and select *Slide Sorter*.
- Move your mouse over a slide that you want to move. Click once and hold.
- Drag the slide where you want to place it and then release the mouse button.
- Repeat for any other slides that you want to move.

▣ Notes Page View

This exciting function of *PowerPoint* allows you to add notes that will only be visible on the printed page. The notes will not be visible in the slide show.

- Click on **Notes Page View** or pull down the **VIEW** menu and select *Notes Page*.
- Move your mouse to the Notes section at the bottom of the page.
- Type notes in the text section.

PowerPoint Tips and Tricks *(cont.)*

Slide Show

Presenting Your Slide Show

When you are ready to present a slide show, you want the slides to be in **Slide Show** format.

- If you are in **Slide View**, scroll to the first slide. If you are in **Slide Sorter View**, select the first slide with your mouse.
- Click on the **Slide Show** icon or pull down the **VIEW** menu and select *Slide Show*.
- To manually transition to the next slide, click the mouse button anywhere on the screen. After you have completed your presentation, your slide show will return either to **Slide View** or **Slide Sorter View**, depending on where you started.

Timing your Slide Show Transitions

- Pull down the **SLIDE SHOW** menu and select *Slide Transition*.
- Move the mouse to the **Advance** box and select the **Automatically after** box.
- Underneath it, type in the number of seconds you want each slide to appear on the screen before transitioning to the next slide.
- Click **Apply to All**.

Making the Slide Show Loop Continuously

- Pull down the **SLIDE SHOW** menu and select *Set Up Show*.
- Select **Loop continuously until 'Esc.'**
- Click **OK**.
- NOTE: Be sure to put in timed transitions or your slide show won't move without a mouse click.
- Press the **Esc** key to end the continuous loop.

PowerPoint Tips and Tricks *(cont.)*

Changing Slide Show Colors

PowerPoint has standard colors for backgrounds, fills, lines, shadows, text, etc. You can change the standard color scheme for any new slide show, or any of the templates in this book. Follow the simple directions below to make any changes. These are also some good tips and tricks you can teach your students so they can make their slide shows even more individualized.

- Pull down the **FORMAT** menu and select *Slide Color Scheme*. Click on the **Custom** tab.
- Move your mouse over the color you want to change and click once. Then click the **Change color** button.
- A honeycomb of colors will appear. Select your desired color.
- Click **OK** and you will return to the original pop-up menu where you click **Apply to All**.
- Repeat these steps to change the standard colors for any slide show presentation.

WordArt and Graphics

Using WordArt

PowerPoint has a very exciting feature: WordArt. This option allows you to create fun and exciting-looking fonts with just the click of a button. Words can be wavy, vertical…or whatever you decide!

- Pull down the **VIEW** menu, go to *Toolbars* and make sure that your *Drawing Toolbar* is selected.
- Click on the **Insert WordArt** icon.
- Select a type of WordArt format that you like and click **OK**.
- Type your text in the pop-up text box.
- Click **OK**.
- The WordArt will appear on the screen. Resize it by selecting the box, clicking on the handles (one of the boxes around the box) and dragging it to the size you prefer.

PowerPoint Tips and Tricks *(cont.)*

Changing WordArt Color

As we mentioned, WordArt can be a fun way to create fonts on your slide. You can choose a font style and color with the click of a button. Changing the color of your WordArt can be just as easy!

- Select your WordArt graphic with your mouse.
- Pull down the **FORMAT** menu and select **WordArt**.
- Click on the **Color and Lines** tab at the top of the dialog box.
- Choose a Fill Color. Check out all the Fill Effects for something really different.
- Choose a Line Color.
- Click **OK**.

Adding a Graphic

Adding graphics to your *PowerPoint* presentations helps make them more exciting and interesting. *PowerPoint* provides a lot of graphics for you and your students to use. To find and use specific graphics, reference the Internet Mini-Lesson on page 13.

- Pull down the **INSERT** menu and select *Picture*.
- From Picture, you have two options: *Clip Art* and *From File*. If you want to use a *PowerPoint* pre-made graphic, select *Clip Art*.
- Scroll through the Clip Art and use your mouse to select a graphic you like.
- Click **Insert** to place it on your slide.
- To retrieve a picture from the Internet, CD, or other source, select *From File*.
- Locate your graphic file and select it with your mouse.
- Click **Insert** to place it on your slide.

Resizing a Graphic

It is simple to take a graphic in *PowerPoint* and either enlarge it to fill the whole slide or reduce it to cover only a small corner. To change your graphic size:

- Select the graphic with your mouse by moving your mouse over the graphic and clicking once.
- Handles will appear around the graphic.
- Move your mouse over one of the handles. You will see the mouse cursor change to a different type of arrow.
- Click on one of the handles and drag it smaller or larger.
- Repeat until you have resized the graphic to your specifications.

PowerPoint Tips & Tricks *(cont.)*

More Fun Features

Making Watermarks

To make your slides more interesting and exciting, you can add a watermark as a background or on a corner of any of your slides. This is especially suitable for a school or district logo if you are making a presentation to parents or teachers.

- Pull down the **INSERT** menu, select *Picture*, and *Clip Art* or *From File*.
- Move your mouse to a piece of clip art you want to use as your Watermark.
- Select the graphic with your mouse and click **Insert**.
- Pull down the **VIEW** menu, select *Toolbars*, and make sure that the *Picture* toolbar is selected.
- Select the **Image Control** icon on the Picture toolbar and click on *Watermark*.
- Use the mouse to select your graphic and the handles to move or resize your watermark.

Using Different Bullet Styles

Many of the presentations you and your students create require bullets to highlight important information. *PowerPoint* has hundreds of fun and exciting symbols that can be used instead of regular bullets. Follow these simple instructions:

- Click once to select the bulleted text box. Highlight what you want to change.
- Pull down the **FORMAT** menu and select *Bullet*.
- A pop-up menu will appear. Click on the arrow next to Normal Text to see all the options.
- Select *Monotype Sorts* from the pulldown menu.
- Click on any bullet to see an enlarged view.
- Once you have found a bullet you like, click on it and then click **OK**.

Adding Animation

PowerPoint allows you to create text that flies, flashes, or disappears from the screen at the click of a button. This is a fun presentation technique that will really interest your students!

- Use your mouse to select a text box or WordArt.
- Pull down the **SLIDE SHOW** menu and select *Preset Animation*.
- Choose an animation from the pop-up menu.
- Run your slide show to see how you like it. Test all the animations to see which one you like best.

PowerPoint Tips & Tricks *(cont.)*

Saving Your Presentation as a Web Page

PowerPoint presentations are easy to place on the Web! All you need to do is save the presentation as an HTML file and upload it up to a class or school Web site. *PowerPoint* has the following simple pop-up menus to help you do this:

- Pull down the **FILE** menu and select *Save as HTML*.

- On the popup dialog box, move your mouse to the **Next** button and click once.

- If you are working on a PC and have saved a presentation as an HTML before, you can use the format of those presentations by selecting **Load existing layout**. If you are saving a presentation as an HTML for the first time, click on **New Layout**. Click the **Next** button.

- Choose either the **Standard** or **Browser** frame from this menu. The Standard frame will give you *PowerPoint*'s standard HTML layout and the Browser frame will let the reader see the outline and notes format along with the slide. Only select the **Browser** frame if you or your students have utilized the outline and notes of the *PowerPoint* presentation. Click **Next**.

- Choose either the **GIF** or **JPEG** way of saving graphics from this menu. Click **Next**.

- Choose the monitor resolution from the menu at the top and the width of the graphic from the pull down menu. Click **Next**.

- You can add your e-mail address or the address of your home page to this pop-up menu. This will give the reader of the *PowerPoint* presentation the ability to contact you with a single click. Enter the information and click **Next**.

- You can either use the standard colors of your browser by selecting **Use browser colors** or you can customize your colors by selecting **Custom Colors**. Make your selection and click **Next**.

- Select the type of buttons you like and click **Next**.

- This screen allows you to decide where you want the buttons placed on your slide show so it is easy for somebody to navigate their way through your presentation. Make your selection of button locations and click **Next**.

- Move your mouse to the **Select** or **Browse** button to decide where you want to save your file. Locate the folder and click **Select**. Click **Next**.

- You have finished creating the defaults for your *PowerPoint* presentation as an HTML file. Click **Finish**.

- You will be told that you have saved your presentation as an HTML file. Click **OK**.

An Internet Mini-Lesson

The Internet contains a wealth of information and photographs that can be utilized when creating a *PowerPoint* presentation. It is important to remember and to remind your students that the Internet is a resource like an encyclopedia or another book they would get out of the library. It needs to be treated like a book and properly cited at all times in bibliographies. Many web sites feature graphics that students can use in their *PowerPoint* presentations, but they cannot use these graphics without the permission of the site's creator.

The great thing about the Internet is that you can send a quick e-mail to get permission to use the photographs. All sites have a webmaster listed at the bottom of the Web page whom a student can e-mail. Students should send a quick e-mail to the webmaster explaining the project they are creating and requesting permission to use the photograph from the site in their presentation (see the sample e-mails on page 15). I have never come across a webmaster from any site who wasn't happy to give their permission to use a photograph in a student-generated presentation. This is especially important if you are planning on posting any of the presentations on a Web site.

Teacher Tip: If you are worried about students using the Internet or wasting too much time searching it, take some time to gather pictures from the Web yourself. Request permission from the webmaster and have all the pictures ready for the students in a folder.

An Internet Mini-lesson *(cont.)*

Capturing a Picture from the Internet

Taking a picture off the Internet is especially easy. If you are using a PC, move the mouse directly over the picture. Right-click on the mouse and a pop-up menu will appear. Move the mouse to select **Save Image As**. A pop-up menu will appear and you can save the image anywhere on the computer.

On a Macintosh machine, move the mouse directly over the picture. Click and hold the mouse down. A pop-up menu will appear. Move the mouse to select **Download Image to Disk**. A pop-up menu will appear and you can save the image anywhere on the computer.

If you are going to insert the image immediately into a *PowerPoint* presentation and then delete it, just save it on the desktop. If you are planning on having your students collect a couple of pictures for their presentation before they begin, then set up a folder. For example, if you class will be working on the Native American Report and they are collecting Native American photographs, create a folder for Native American pictures that your students can use in their presentations.

Sites Which Offer Free Graphics

The following sites have samples of graphics to use on your page and help in choosing background colors for your pages. You are encouraged to save and use these graphics and incorporate them into your page.

Animated Graphics Gallery

http://www.geocities.com/SiliconValley/Pines/9466/index.html
This gallery has over 1,000 animated GIFs for your pages. The author has divided the graphics into categories to make the searching easier.

Barry's Clip Art Links

http://www.barrysclipart.com/links/links.html
This most comprehensive list of clip art sites on the Net is classified by subject.

Clip Art Connection

http://www.clipartconnection.com/index.html
This is an image archive of custom backgrounds, horizontal rules, animated globes, decorative lettering and much more.

Jelane's Free Web Graphics

http://www.erinet.com/jelane/families/
Coordinating sets of free graphics for your Web pages contain a background edge, horizontal rule, home, e–mail, links, blank buttons, and a bullet. A great site!

Library Clip Art Collection

http://www.JanetMeyers.com/clipart.html
GIFS of books, computers, and library-related topics are there for you to use.

Sample e-mail #1

Send this to a webmaster if you are not planning on putting any of your presentations on a classroom or school Web site.

Dear Webmaster,

My name is Corinne. I am a third grader at Oak Grove Elementary School in Aliso Viejo, CA. In my class, we are making a *PowerPoint* presentation on Native Americans. You have some very nice pictures of Native Americans on your site.

I was wondering if I could use some of your pictures from your site in my *PowerPoint* presentation. The presentation will only be used in my school. I will be sure to cite your Web site as a reference in my bibliography. Please let me know if it will be all right for me to use your pictures.

Thank you,

Corinne Burton

Sample e-mail #2

Send this to a webmaster if you are planning on putting your presentation on a classroom or school web site.

Dear Webmaster,

My name is Corinne. I am a third grader at Oak Grove Elementary School in Aliso Viejo, CA. In my class we are making a *PowerPoint* presentation on Native Americans. You have some very nice pictures of Native Americans on your site.

I was hoping to use some of your pictures from your site in my presentation. We will be using the site in our classroom and posting it on our classroom/school Web site so our parents and other students can see my presentation. I will be sure to cite your Web site as a reference in my bibliography. Please let me know if it will be all right for me to use your pictures.

Thank you,

Corinne Burton

Assessing a Presentation

When assessing a *PowerPoint* presentation, it is important to remember to encourage your students to continue to explore and experiment on the computer. Look for students who are willing to explore new concepts and develop new types of presentations. Below are some sample rubrics you can use in your assessment.

Name: _____

Title of Presentation: _____

Content	Good	Better	Best
Demonstrates knowledge of topic			
Text is clear and easy to understand			
Text has few grammar and spelling errors			

Presentation	Good	Better	Best
Slides are well organized			
Slides are free of extra clutter			
Presentation follows a sequential path			

Name: _____

Title of Presentation: _____

Knowledgeable about topic _____ (25 points)

Grammar and spelling is correct _____ (25 points)

Slides are well organized _____ (25 points)

Presentation is sequential _____ (25 points)

Total points _____ (100 points)

Assessing a Presentation *(cont.)*

Name:

Title of Presentation:

Dear _____,

I really enjoyed your *PowerPoint* presentation.

My favorite part of the slide show was

Your slides were

Your text was

Next time you create a slide show, remember to

Your presentation of your slide show was

Next time you do a presentation, remember to

Sincerely,

_____

Assessing a Presentation *(cont.)*

Here is an example of how to fill out the assessment on p. 17.

Name: *Joey*

Title of Presentation: *The Chumash Indians*

Dear _____*Joey*_____,

I really enjoyed your *PowerPoint* presentation.

My favorite part of the slide show was *all the interesting information about the clothing of the Chumash Indians. I had no idea how they dressed. Thank you for teaching me.*

Your slides were *well organized. It was easy for me to see all the information you wanted to show.*

Your text was *clear and fun to read. I really appreciate all the extra time you took to make sure there weren't any spelling or grammar errors!*

Next time you create a slide show, remember to *make sure that everybody can read the text boxes. It is a good idea to make the text color a lot different from the background color.*

Your presentation of your slide show was *fun, and it was exciting to hear all the new information.*

Next time you do a presentation, remember to *speak clearly and face the audience.*

Sincerely,

Mrs. Burton

Postcards

This Project

In this project, your students will create a postcard from a place they might have visited over a break or weekend. The emphasis of this lesson will be on designing an exciting picture to entice the postcard recipient to flip the slide and read about the location. Students will be encouraged to write an exciting description full of factual and interesting information about the location.

Computer Skills

- Adding graphics to a slide

- Designing graphics for a slide

- Adding text to a slide

Before Beginning

- Discuss with students some different places they have visited recently. Remind them to choose a place they can describe in great detail and about which they can create a picture. Be sure to tell them that they can write a fun and exciting postcard from a local amusement park or beach if they wish.

- Have each student complete the Student Planning Page on page 22. A good warm-up activity for them would be to watch you fill out information on the Student Planning Sheet about some place you visited over the break. You could either put the planning sheet on an overhead or recreate it on a board to be filled out.

- Show students how to locate the template for this project.

Quick Steps

- Open the *PowerPoint* template called (*Postcard*).

- Use the text, paint, and graphic tools to create a postcard scene inside the box.

- Move to the next slide.

- On the second slide, insert the text from your postcard in the text area.

- Insert the address to which you are sending the postcard in the address area.

- Go to the clip art menu and choose a piece of clip art for your stamp. Resize it so that it fits in the stamp box in the upper right hand corner.

- Save and print your postcard.

Postcards *(cont.)*

Procedure

Step 1   Open *PowerPoint* and select **Open an Existing Presentation**. Click **OK**.

Step 2   A pop-up box with all the files will appear on the screen. Select
(*Postcard*) and click **Open**.

Step 3   On the first slide, you will need to design the front of your postcard with a picture that
encourages the receiver to read it. Check to make sure that the Drawing toolbar is on the
screen. If it is not, pull down the **VIEW** menu, select *Toolbars* and choose the *Drawing*
toolbar.

Step 4   Move your mouse to the rectangle drawn on your slide. Click on the rectangle so that it is
selected. Then move your mouse to the **Fill Color** tool on the Drawing tool bar. (*Hint:* If
you aren't sure which tool is which, slowly move your mouse over the icons and the name of
each tool will pop up on the screen.)

Step 5   Click on the arrow to the right of the **Fill Color** tool, then click on **More Fill Colors** from the
pop-up menu. Choose from the many colors available to select a background for your
postcard. Click **OK**.

Step 6   Pull down the **INSERT** menu, select *Picture*, and choose *Clip Art*. Scroll through the
available clip art and select pictures you would like to put on the front of your postcard.
Highlight your selection with the mouse and click **Insert**.

Step 7   To add a picture from another source, pull down the **INSERT** menu, select *Picture*, and
choose *From File*. Scroll through the files until you find where you have saved your desired
graphic and click **Insert** to add it to your postcard.

Step 8   Use the mouse pointer to resize the picture if necessary. Move your mouse arrow to the
edges (boxes) of the graphic and drag to the size needed.

Step 9   Pull down the **INSERT** menu and select *Text Box*. A pointer will appear on the screen. Use
the mouse to draw a box indicating where you want the text to appear.

Step 10   Select a size and style of font that you like and type some sort of catchy message that would
make the receiver of the postcard want to read more. When you are finished, click outside the
box. Use the mouse to move the text if necessary.

Step 11   Use the scroll bar on the right hand side of the screen to move down to the next screen.

Step 12   Use the mouse to click on the address section of the postcard and follow the directions in the
box.

Step 13   Use the mouse to click on the letter portion of the postcard. Erase the text in the box and
write your letter.

Step 14   Pull down the **INSERT** menu, select *Picture*, and choose *Clip Art*. Scroll through the
available clip art and find the picture you would like for your stamp. Once you have found
your graphic, select it with the mouse and click Insert.

Postcards *(cont.)*

Step 15   When it pops in, the graphic will probably cover a large portion of the page. Use your mouse to resize the graphic and move it into the stamp box.

Step 16   Pull down the **FILE** menu and select *Save As*. Make sure that you are saving it to a folder where you can find it later. Give your file the name (*your name Postcard*). Click the **Save** button.

Step 17   Pull down the **FILE** menu and select *Print*. Click **OK** (PC) or **Print** (Mac) to print a hard copy of your postcard.

Postcards *(cont.)*

Student Planning Page

You are going to be writing a postcard to a friend or family member from a place you visited over the break. Think about some fun and exciting things that happened to you on your vacation and fill out the information below.

On my vacation I went

_____

_____

_____

My favorite thing I saw was

_____

_____

_____

The most fun thing I did was

_____

_____

_____

I went on my vacation with

_____

_____

_____

I would like to send a postcard to

_____

_____

_____

Story Sequencing

This Project

In this project, your students will trace the sequence of events in a story they have read. Using an organization chart format, they will identify the key events from a piece of literature and place them on an organization chart in the order in which they occurred.

Computer Skills

- Adding graphics
- Adding and using text frames
- Organizing text frames on a slide

Before Beginning

- Each student will read a book of his/her own choice. They will use the reading log on page 25 to note the main characters, setting, and four main events as they happen. This will provide a chronology for the story.
- Review what defines a main character versus a secondary character.
- Review the definition of setting.
- Show students how to locate the template for this project.

Quick Steps

- Open the *PowerPoint* template called (*Story*).
- Move the mouse to the title and click to write the name of your story.
- Move the mouse to the Main Characters box, click on the box and type the names of the main characters.
- Move the mouse to the Setting box and write a couple of sentences describing the setting of your book.
- Move the mouse to the box that says First. Complete the sentence describing the first main event of the story.
- Select the Next, Then, and Finally boxes and complete the sentences.
- Pull down the **FORMAT** menu to change the colors and look of your slide.
- Pull down the **INSERT** menu and select *Picture* to add a graphic to your slide.
- Save and print your work.

Story Sequencing *(cont.)*

Procedure

Step 1   Open the *PowerPoint* template (*Story*).

Step 2   Move the mouse to the large box at the top where it states "Click to add title." Click on the box to write the name of your story and the name of the author.

Step 3   Move the mouse to the first box titled Main Characters and double-click on it.

Step 4   Use your mouse to move to the end of the Main Characters title. Press the **Return** or **Enter** key and list the main characters of the story.

Step 5   Once you have finished typing, select the box with your mouse. Move your mouse over one of the squares on the corners of the box. Click and drag to resize it. You will need to repeat this after you fill in each text box.

Step 6   Move the mouse to the next text box titled Setting. Select it and include a couple of sentences that describe the setting of your story.

Step 7   Repeat Step 6 for the Next box, the Then box and the Finally box. Describe the next three events in the story by completing these boxes.

Step 8   If you need to add more events to your story, pull down the **INSERT** menu and select *Text Box*. An I-beam will appear. Click and type to add these events. Repeat as often as necessary to add the boxes you need. If you do not need to use a box, select it with the mouse and push the **Delete** key.

Step 9   To change your background, pull down the **FORMAT** menu and select *Background*. Move to the bottom of the Background Fill menu and click once on the arrow. Then select **More Colors**.

Step 10   A honeycomb of colors appears. Select a color, click **OK** and then **Apply**.

Step 11   To change your font, click and drag to highlight the text you want to change. Pull down the **FORMAT** menu and select *Font*. Choose a font you like.

Step 12   Pull down the **INSERT** menu and select *Picture*. Choose a picture that coincides with your story for the slide. Insert the picture and place it on your slide.

Step 13   Pull down the **FILE** menu and select *Save As*. Change the filename to (*Story your initials*). Click **OK**.

Step 14   Pull down the **FILE** menu and select *Print*. Click **OK** (PC) or **Print** (Mac).

Story Sequencing

Student Planning Page

Reading Log

Choose a book to read. Read the story once and then go back and reread the story. While rereading the story, fill out the reading log below.

Name:

Title of Book or Story:

Author of Book or Story:

Main Characters:

First,

Next,

Then,

Finally,

In the box, write a short summary of the story.

Sell the Book

This Project

In this project, your students will design a single slide to advertise a book they have read. They will try to highlight the most interesting parts of the book so people will want to run out and read it.

Computer Skills

- Using text boxes
- Using WordArt
- Adding graphics

Before the Computer

- Show your students some sample book advertisements from magazines. Mention that most of these ads include a graphic, a book title, and a summary or some quotes about the book.
- Show students how to locate the template for this project.
- Have your students complete the Student Planning Page on page 29.

Teacher Extensions

- Once all the students have printed out their slides, bind them into a book they can flip through when deciding which book to choose for free reading.
- Assemble the finished slides into a slide show that students can reference when they need to find good books. See instructions on page 28 on how to tie individual slides together into one teacher-created slide show.
- Leave these instructions near your computer the entire year. When a student finishes a book they like, they can create a slide to advertise it to the rest of the class.

Quick Steps

- Open *PowerPoint* and select the (*Book*) template.
- Double-click on the top of the page and add the title of your book. You can use the WordArt functions to change the shape of your title.
- Click on the quote text box and write an exciting quote for your book.
- Click on the summary text box at the bottom of the page and write a two-to three-sentence summary of your book.
- Double-click on the graphic to add a *PowerPoint* graphic that is appropriate for your story.
- You can use the text box tool to add more quotes to your slide.
- Save and print your slide.
- Repeat this process for the Setting, Characters, Plot, and Recommmendation slides.

Sell the Book (cont.)

Procedure

Step 1   Open *PowerPoint* and select **Open an existing presentation**. Click **OK**.

Step 2   A pop-up box with all the files will appear on the screen. Select (*Book*) and click the **Open** button.

Step 3   Move the mouse to the top of the slide and double-click on Title of the Book Here.

Step 4   When the test box pops up, type the name of your book in the box and select **OK**.

Step 5   Move the mouse to the text box that asks for a quote. Click on the box and delete the writing inside the box. Write your quote inside the box. Be sure to press **Return** when it's time to start a new line.

Step 6   Move the mouse to the text box that asks for a summary. Click on the box and delete the writing inside the box. Write a 2-3-sentence summary of your book inside the summary text box.

Step 7   Move the mouse to the graphic. Double-click on the Snowman graphic. Scroll through the available *PowerPoint* graphics and select one to fit your book. Click **OK**.

Step 8   Pull down the **FILE** menu and select *Save As*. Give your file the name (*Book Title your initials*).

Step 9   Repeat the steps above for the additional slides provided. Include the information requested on each slide.

Step 10   To print your slides, pull down the **FILE** menu and select *Print*. Click **OK** (PC) or **Print** (Mac) and print your advertisement!

Step 11   Present your slide show to the class.

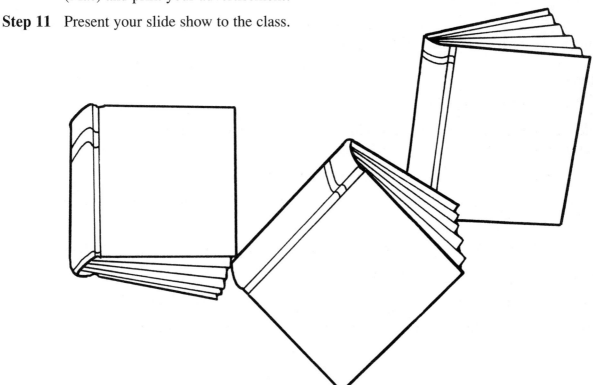

Sell the Book *(cont.)*

Teacher Instructions for Making a *PowerPoint* Slide Show

Step 1 Once all the students have completed their slides, open *PowerPoint*, choose **Blank Presentation** and click **OK**. The New Slide dialog box will appear; click **Cancel**.

Step 2 Pull down the **INSERT** menu and select *Slides From Files*. If you are working on a PC, move your mouse to the **Browse** button and click once.

Step 3 Scroll through your files and locate the student slide you want to place first in your electronic slide show.

Step 4 Select the file with your mouse and click **Open** (PC) or **Insert** (Mac).

Step 5 If you are working on a PC, the file name will appear in the File box. Click **Display**. A picture of the slide will appear in the box below.

Step 6 Continue repeating Steps 2-5 for each slide you want to place in your slide show.

Step 7 If you are working on a PC and have selected all your slides, move your mouse to the **Insert All** button and click once.

Step 8 Move your mouse to the **Close** button and click once.

Step 9 Pull down the **VIEW** menu and select *Slide Sorter* to rearrange the slides in any order that you want (i.e. alphabetical order).

Step 10 Pull down the **FILE** menu and select *Save As*. Give your file the name (*your name sell*).

Step 11 Pull down the **FILE** menu and select *Print*. Click **OK** (PC) or **Print** (Mac).

Sell the Book *(cont.)*

Student Planning Page

You have just read a great book. You want to try and sell it to other readers. Your goal is to make it look interesting and sound fascinating so that people will want to run out and read it.

Title of Book: _____

_____

Write a two-to three-sentence summary of your book. _____

_____

_____

_____

Use your summary to think of a phrase to make your book sound exciting. Remember that a phrase is not a complete sentence; it is just a couple of words to show a quick idea.

_____

_____

_____

Sketch a picture you might want to use on your advertisement. When you create it on the computer, you can either use the drawing tools or insert a pre-made graphic.

Electronic Yearbook

This Project

In this project, students will create a single slide including their picture and a short biography describing their accomplishments for the year. All student slides will be combined into a single slide show presentation about the entire class. This is a good project to show at Open House.

Computer Skills

- Adding graphics to a slide
- Adding text boxes to a slide
- Using a digital camera or scanning pictures into a computer

Before Beginning

- Take a picture of each student in your class. Then take a picture of the entire class. Scan the pictures into the computer, or if you used a digital camera, download them onto the computer.
- Have your students vote on a title for their Electronic Yearbook.
- Have students complete the Student Planning Page on page 34. Show them how to fill it out by completing one for yourself.
- Show students how to locate the template for this project.

Teacher Extensions

- Send students home with a printed or electronic format of their class yearbook.

Quick Steps: Student Yearbook Instructions

- Open a blank *PowerPoint* presentation.
- Select a background color for your slide.
- Insert a picture of yourself. Using your mouse, resize it as necessary.
- Insert a text box describing what you accomplished this year. Resize it to fit the slide.
- Save the slide with your name and print it.

Quick Steps: Teacher Yearbook Instructions

- Once all the students have finished their slides, open the (*Yearbook*) template.
- Move your mouse over the title of the WordArt and double-click. Change the name.
- Double-click on the dates at the bottom of the screen to change them.
- Insert a picture of the entire class for the opening slide.
- Pull down the **INSERT** menu and select *Slides From Files*. Click on **Browse**.
- Scroll through your files to locate a student's slide. Click **Open** and then click **Display**.
- Repeat for every student's slide.
- Once completed, click **Insert All** and then **Close**.
- Save and print your completed yearbook.

Electronic Yearbook *(cont.)*

Student Instructions

Step 1   Open *PowerPoint* and select a **Blank Presentation**. Click **OK**.

Step 2   The AutoLayout menu will appear. Select a **Blank Slide** and click **OK**.

Step 3   Pull down the **FORMAT** menu and select *Background*.

Step 4   Move your mouse to the arrow at the bottom of the Background Fill menu and click once on the menu.

Step 5   Select **More Colors** with your mouse.

Step 6   A honeycomb of colors will appear. Select a color you like for your slide background.

Step 7   Click **OK**. On the second menu, click **Apply**.

Step 8   Pull down the **INSERT** menu. Select *Picture*, and *From File*. Locate the picture of yourself in your files.

Step 9   Select the picture file and click **Insert**.

Step 10   Use the mouse and handles to resize your graphic as necessary.

Step 11   Pull down the **INSERT** menu and select *Text Box*.

Step 12   Use the mouse to move the I-beam to the location where you want your text box. Click once for a text box to appear.

Step 13   Using the Student Planning Page as a guide, type a paragraph describing your accomplishments and favorite activities for this year. Be sure to press **Return** to keep the text box on the slide.

Step 14   Use the mouse and handles to resize your text box as necessary.

Step 15   Pull down the **FILE** menu and select *Save As*. Give your file the name (*your name year*).

Step 16   Pull down the **FILE** menu and select *Print*. Click **OK** (PC) or **Print** (Mac).

Electronic Yearbook *(cont.)*

Teacher Instructions

Step 1 Once all the students have completed their slides, open *PowerPoint* and select **Open an existing presentation**.

Step 2 Select the (*Yearbook*) template and click **Open**.

Step 3 Move your mouse until it is over the title at the top of the page and double-click on it.

Step 4 A pop-up text box menu will appear. Highlight and delete the text in the box and give your class yearbook a title.

Step 5 Move your mouse over the dates on the bottom of the page and double-click on them.

Step 6 A pop-up text box menu will appear. Highlight and delete the text in the box and put in the dates of the current school year.

Step 7 Pull down the **INSERT** menu. Select *Picture*, and *From Files*.

Step 8 Locate the picture of the entire class that you either scanned or downloaded into the computer.

Step 9 Select the picture with the mouse and click **Insert**.

Step 10 Using the mouse and handles, resize the graphic as necessary.

Step 11 Pull down the **INSERT** menu and select *Slides From Files*.

Step 12 If you are working on a PC, move your mouse to the **Browse** button and click once.

Step 13 Scroll through your files and locate the student you want to place first in your electronic yearbook.

Step 14 Select the file with your mouse and click **Open** (PC) or **Insert** (Mac).

Step 15 If you are working on a PC, the file name will appear in the File box. Click **Display**. A picture of the slide will appear in the box below.

Step 16 Repeat Steps 13–15 for each student in your class.

Step 17 If you are working on a PC and have selected all the student pictures, click on Insert All. Move your mouse to the **Close** button and click on it.

Step 18 Pull down the **VIEW** menu and select *Slide Sorter* to rearrange the slides in any order you please (such as alphabetical order).

Step 19 Pull down the **FILE** menu and select *Save As*. Give your file the name (your name yrbk).

Step 20 Pull down the **FILE** menu and select *Print*. Click **OK** (PC) or **Print** (Mac).

Electronic Yearbook *(cont.)*

Teresa Burton

This year in school I came in second place in the Spelling Bee. I would have gotten first place, but I forgot to say "capital F" for February.

Electronic Yearbook *(cont.)*

Student Planning Page

Think back over the school year about some of the fabulous things you have accomplished. Answer the questions below. Use this as a guide to write a paragraph about the things you remember most about this school year.

Name: _____

1. My most favorite project was _____

_____

_____

2. The funniest things that happened this year was_____

_____

_____

3. The best thing I did in school was _____

_____

_____

4. The best thing I did outside of school was_____

_____

_____

5. My best friends are_____

_____

_____

6. I will never forget _____

_____

_____

All About Me

This Project

In this project, your students will create a slide show presentation documenting their lives thus far. Students will add pictures of themselves at various stages and include text to tell stories about that time. This is a good activity to encourage students in their storytelling skills.

Computer Skills

- Scanning graphics into the computer
- Adding graphics to a slide
- Adding text to a slide
- Creating a coherent slide show presentation

Before Beginning

- Tell students they are going to be creating a slide show about their lives.
- With their parents' permission, have each student collect pictures of himself or herself as a baby, preschooler, kindergartner, and at least two grades past kindergarten.
- Scan these pictures into the computer and place them in a folder on the desktop for the students to access. I suggest saving each picture by the student's name followed by a number representing his or her age at that time.
- Have students complete the Student Planning Page on page 37 at home with their parents.
- This is a good project to send home with them on holidays such as Christmas, Hanukkah, Mother's Day, or Father's Day.

Quick Steps

- Open a Blank *PowerPoint* Presentation.
- Select a Background color for your slide show.
- Add a WordArt title with your name and date of birth.
- Insert a picture of you as a baby.
- Add a text box and tell a story from the time when you were a baby.
- Add a new slide.
- Add a WordArt title that says Preschool.
- Insert a picture of you as a preschooler.
- Add a text box and tell a story from the time when you were a preschooler.
- Add a new slide.
- Repeat the above steps for slides about kindergarten and two more school years.
- Save and Print.

All About Me *(cont.)*

Procedure

Step 1   Open *PowerPoint* and select a **Blank Presentation**. Click **OK**.

Step 2   From the AutoLayout menu, select a **Blank slide** and click **OK**.

Step 3   Pull down the **FORMAT** menu and select *Background*. Pull down the arrow on the pop-up menu and select **More Colors**.

Step 4   A honeycomb of colors will appear. Select your color, click **OK** and then click **Apply to All**.

Step 5   Pull down the **VIEW** menu, select *Toolbars* and choose the *Drawing* toolbar.

Step 6   Click on the **WordArt** icon, select a type of WordArt and click **OK**.

Step 7   A pop-up text box will appear. Type in your name and your date of birth in the text box. Click **OK**.

Step 8   Using the mouse, move the WordArt title to the top of the slide and resize it with the handles.

Step 9   Pull down the **INSERT** menu, select *Picture*, and *From File*.

Step 10   Locate a picture of you as a baby, select it with the mouse and click **Insert**.

Step 11   Pull down the **INSERT** menu and select *Text Box*.

Step 12   An I-beam will appear on the screen. Click the mouse where you want to place the text box on the slide.

Step 13   In the text box, type a story about yourself as a baby.

Step 14   Use the mouse and the handles to reorganize your slide as necessary.

Step 15   Pull down the **INSERT** menu and select *New Slide*. Click on **Blank** and click **OK**.

Step 16   Click on the **WordArt** icon, select a WordArt type and click **OK**.

Step 17   A pop-up text box will appear. Type (*Preschool*) in the text box. Click **OK**.

Step 18   Using the mouse, move the WordArt title to the top of the slide and resize it with the handles.

Step 19   Pull down the **INSERT** menu, select *Picture*, and *From File*.

Step 20   Locate a picture of you as a preschooler, select it with the mouse and click Insert. Pull down the **INSERT** menu and select *Text box*.

Step 21   An I-beam will appear on the screen. Click the mouse where you want the text box on the slide.

Step 22   In the text box, type a story about yourself as a preschooler.

Step 23   Pull down the **INSERT** menu and select *New Slide*.

Step 24   Repeat Steps 15-23 for your kindergarten year and two other years of school.

Step 25   Pull down the **FILE** menu and select *Save As*.

Step 26   Give your file the name (*your name Me*).

Step 27   Pull down the **FILE** menu and select *Print*. Click **OK** (PC) or **Print** (Mac).

All About Me (cont.)

Student Planning Page

You are going to create a slide show presentation all about your life. Go home and gather some pictures from your childhood. Be sure to get pictures of yourself as a:

- ❑ baby
- ❑ preschooler
- ❑ kindergartner
- ❑ another school year
- ❑ another school year

Think about some of the stories you have heard told or that you remember from those years. If you can't remember any stories, ask your parents to help you out.

When I was a baby, I _____

_____

_____

When I was a preschooler, I_____

_____

_____

When I was a kindergartner, I _____

_____

_____

When I was in _____ grade, I _____

_____

_____

When I was in _____ grade, I _____

_____

_____

National Symbols

This Project

In this project, your students will create a slide show presentation to demonstrate and explain some national symbols. They will need to find exciting pictures of national symbols and write explanations of the historic items.

Computer Skills

- Adding graphics to a slide
- Word processing
- Changing fonts
- Adding text to a slide
- Creating a slide show presentation

Before Beginning

- Complete Internet Mini-Lesson on pages 13–15.
- Some good sites to use are:

    National Portrait Gallery: Hall of Presidents
    http://www.npg.si.edu/col/pres/index.htm

    White House for Kids
    http://www.whitehouse.gov/WH/kids/html/home.html

    Betsy Ross Home Page
    http://www.libertynet.org/iha/betsy/index.html

- Review some important national symbols such as: the U.S. flag, Statue of Liberty, White House, bald eagle, Declaration of Independence, Constitution, and Star Spangled Banner.
- There are a lot of good books for students to read to become acquainted with these symbols:

    All Jean Fritz books are good, especially:
    Shh! We're Writing the Constitution (Putnam, *1987*)
    Will you Sign Here, John Hancock? (Putnam, *1976*)
    Who's that Stepping on Plymouth Rock (Putnam, *1975*)

- Encourage your students to choose their own symbols that they think represent them as Americans. Some good examples are types of music, sports heroes, types of clothes, etc.
- Complete the Student Planning Page on page 41.
- Show students how to locate the template for this project.

Teacher Note: This project can be easily adapted for *PowerPoint* presentations on local or state symbols. A good source of pictures would be local city-and state-sponsored Web sites.

National Symbols *(cont.)*

Quick Steps

- Open the (*National*) template.

- Pull down the **INSERT** menu, select *Picture* and insert a graphic from your national symbols files.

- Insert a text box on the page to add your name as the author.

- Move down to the second slide. Add the name of your national symbol at the top of the page.

- Double-click on the graphic box to add a picture of your symbol.

- Click on the text box to add information about why you think this is a national symbol and when and where you see this symbol. Use your Student Planning Page on page 41 as a guide.

- Repeat the above step for the next two slides, adding information about more national symbols.

- Move to the final slide to add the bibliographical information about the slide show. Remember to cite the Web sites where you got the pictures.

- Save and print your presentation.

- To make the bullets in your text boxes more fun, see page 11 for different bullet styles.

Procedure

Step 1   Open *PowerPoint* and choose **Open an existing presentation**. Click **OK**.

Step 2   Select the *(National)* template. Click **Open**.

Step 3   The first slide has a National Symbols title. On this title page, you need to insert a graphic of a national symbol. Pull down the **INSERT** menu and select *Picture*. If you are using a *PowerPoint* clip art piece, select *Clip Art*. If you are using a graphic from elsewhere, select *From File*.

Step 4   Find the graphic you want and insert it onto the page. Resize the graphic by selecting it and using your mouse on the boxes around the graphic to make the graphic larger or smaller.

Step 5   Pull down the **INSERT** menu and select *Text Box*. Put the text box at the bottom of the page and type your name.

Step 6   Move to the next slide by taking your mouse to the right-hand scroll bar and scrolling down to the next slide.

Step 7   Click on the title line to type the name of your national symbol. You can also use Word Art for your title (See WordArt lesson on page 9).

Step 8   Double-click on the "Double-click to add clip art" box. It will take you to *PowerPoint*'s clip art files. If you want to use a graphic from your files, select **Import Clips** from the bottom of the pop-up screen. Click on the **Insert** button to place the graphic in the slide.

Step 9   Click on the text box on the right side of the screen. In this box, add a couple of short phrases explaining the reasons you think your picture is a national symbol and when and where you would see this symbol.

         NOTE: To make the bullets in your text boxes more fun, see page 11 for different bullet styles.

Step 10   Repeat steps 6-9 for the third and fourth slides.

Step 11   Move to the next slide by taking your mouse to the right-hand scroll bar and scrolling down to the next slide.

Step 12   The final slide of this presentation is a bibliography. Click on the text box to add your bibliographical information. Remember to cite the Web sites where you got the pictures.

Step 13   Pull down the **FILE** menu and select *Save As*. Give your file the name *(Symbols your initials)*.

Step 14   Pull down the **FILE** menu and select *Print*. Click **OK** (PC) or **Print** (Mac).

National Symbols *(cont.)*

Student Planning Page

There are symbols that we as Americans use to help define us as a nation. Think about the things that make you feel as if you are an American. Choose a couple of national symbols and explain what makes them symbols of our country. Explain why an American would feel proud to be an American when they see your symbol.

After you fill in this information, use it to make your slide show presentation.

Symbol: _____

Where would you find this symbol? _____

Why do you think this is a national symbol?_____

How do you feel when you see or hear this symbol?_____

Symbol: _____

Where would you find this symbol? _____

Why do you think this is a national symbol?_____

How do you feel when you see or hear this symbol?_____

Symbol: _____

Where would you find this symbol? _____

Why do you think this is a national symbol?_____

How do you feel when you see or hear this symbol?_____

Native American Report

This Project

In this project, your students will choose a Native American tribe and create a presentation about their culture, shelter, food, and clothing.

Computer Skills

- Adding a graphic to a slide
- Adding a text box to a slide
- Creating a slide show presentation
- Capturing graphics from the Internet

Before Beginning

- Complete Internet Mini-Lesson on page 13-15.
- Have students research the various Native American tribes they will include in their reports.
- The following are good Web sites to use for research on Native Americans.

    Index of Native-American Resources on the Internet
    http://www.hanksville.org/NAresources

    Carol Hurst's Children's Literature Site: Native Americans
    http://www.carolhurst.com/subjects/nativeamericans.html

- Show students how to locate the template for this project.
- Have students complete the Student Planning Pages on 46-49.

Quick Steps

- Open the (*Native*) template in *PowerPoint*.
- Change the WordArt title by typing the name of your Native American tribe.
- Insert a picture of your Native American tribe on the cover of your page.
- Insert a text box with your name.
- Scroll down to the second slide, Culture.
- Insert a picture illustrating a cultural fact about your Native American tribe.
- Insert a text box that includes a description of the culture of your tribe.
- Scroll down to the third slide, Shelter.
- Insert a picture illustrating the type of shelter your tribe used.
- Insert a text box to explain the type of shelter your tribe used and why that type of shelter was beneficial to their lifestyle.
- Scroll down to the fourth slide, Food.

Native American Report *(cont.)*

- Insert a picture of the type of food that your tribe ate or how they prepared their food.

- Insert a text box explaining the types of food your tribe ate and how they got their food.

- Scroll down to the fifth slide, Clothing.

- Insert a picture with a member of your tribe in their native clothing.

- Insert a text box explaining the types of clothing your tribe wore and why that type of clothing was appropriate for where they lived.

- Scroll down to the final slide, Bibliography.

- Click on the text box to add your bibliographical information. Be sure to include in your bibliography the Web sites where you found the pictures you used in your presentation.

- Save and print your report.

Native American Report (cont.)

Procedure

Step 1   Open *PowerPoint* and select **Open an existing presentation**. Click **OK**.

Step 2   Locate the (*Native*) template and click **Open**.

Step 3   On slide 1, move your mouse over the WordArt title and double-click.

Step 4   A pop-up text box will appear. Highlight the information in the text box and delete. Type in the name of the Native American tribe you have selected.

Step 5   Pull down the **INSERT** menu, select *Picture*, and *From File*. Search through your files and locate a picture of your Native American tribe you want on your title slide. Click **Insert** to place the picture on the slide.

Step 6   Select the graphic with your mouse and use the mouse and the handles to resize the graphic as needed.

Step 7   Pull down the **INSERT** menu and select *Text Box*. An I-beam will appear on the screen. Click where you want the text box and type in your name.

Step 8   Move your mouse to the right side of the screen and use the scroll bar to move down to the next slide, Culture.

Step 9   Pull down the **INSERT** menu, select *Picture*, and *From File*. Search through your files and locate a picture of your tribe participating in a cultural event. Click **Insert**.

Step 10   Use your mouse and the handles to resize the graphic.

Step 11   Pull down the **INSERT** menu and select *Text Box*.

Step 12   Move the I-beam on the screen to where you want the text box and click once. Type a paragraph explaining the culture of your tribe.

Step 13   Move your mouse to the right side of the screen and use the scroll bar to move down to the next slide, Shelter.

Step 14   Pull down the **INSERT** menu, select *Picture*, and *From File*. Search through your files and locate a picture of the type of shelter that your tribe used. Click **Insert**.

Step 15   Use your mouse and the handles to resize the graphic.

Step 16   Pull down the **INSERT** menu and select *Text box*.

Step 17   Move the I-beam on the screen to where you want the text box and click once. Type a paragraph explaining the type of shelter your tribe used and why it was beneficial to your tribe.

Step 18   Move your mouse to the right side of the screen and use the scroll bar to move down to the next slide, Food.

Step 19   Pull down the **INSERT** menu, select *Picture*, and *From File*. Search through your files and locate a picture of the types of foods that your tribe ate or a picture of the tribe preparing, gathering, or growing food. Click **Insert**.

Step 20   Use your mouse and the handles to resize the graphic.

Step 21   Pull down the **INSERT** menu and select *Text box*.

Step 22   Move the I-beam on the screen to where you want the text box and click once. Type a paragraph explaining the types of food your tribe ate and how they got their food.

Step 23 Move your mouse to the right side of the screen and use the scroll bar to move down to the next slide, Clothing.

Step 24 Pull down the **INSERT** menu, select *Picture*, and *From File*. Search through your files to locate a picture of a member of your tribe dressed in their native clothing.

Step 25 Use your mouse and the handles to resize the graphic as needed on your slide.

Step 26 Pull down the **FILE** menu and select *Text Box*.

Step 27 Move the I-beam on the screen to where you want the text box and click once. Type a paragraph explaining the types of clothes your tribe wore and why they were appropriate for where they lived.

Step 28 Move your mouse to the right side of the screen and use the scroll bar to move down to the final slide, Bibliography.

Step 29 Move your mouse over the text box on the screen and click once to add bibliographical information. Add the names of any books and web sites you used in your presentation.

Step 30 Pull down the **FILE** menu and select *Save As*. Give your file the name (*name of your tribe your initials*).

Step 31 Pull down the **FILE** menu and select *Print*. Click **OK** (PC) or **Print** (Mac).

Native American Report *(cont.)*

Student Planning Page: Culture

Name: _____

Name of your Native American Tribe: _____

List ten interesting facts about the culture of your tribe.

1. _____
2. _____
3. _____
4. _____
5. _____
6. _____
7. _____
8. _____
9. _____
10. _____

Do you think you would have liked living with your Native American tribe? Why or why not?

_____

_____

_____

_____

_____

_____

Native American Report *(cont.)*

Student Planning Page: Shelter

Draw a picture below of the type of shelter used by your tribe.

What is the name of this type of shelter?_____

Why was this type of shelter used by your tribe?_____

_____

_____

_____

Native American Report *(cont.)*

Student Planning Page: Food

How did your tribe get food to eat? _____

_____

_____

_____

List at least ten types of food that Native Americans from your tribe would eat.

1. _____

2. _____

3. _____

4. _____

5. _____

6. _____

7. _____

8. _____

9. _____

10. _____

Native American Report *(cont.)*

Student Planning Page: Clothing

Draw a picture below of the way a man, woman, and child from your tribe would have looked.

Man	Woman	Child

How did your tribe make clothing? _____

_____

_____

How did your tribe's clothing reflect the area where they were living? _____

_____

_____

_____

Family Tree

This Project

In this project, your students will research their family genealogy and record their findings in a family tree. Students will make their family tree using an Organizational Chart slide in *PowerPoint*.

Computer Skills

- Organizational Charts

Before Beginning

- Discuss with students what a family tree is.

- Have students take home the Student Planning Page on page 52. Inform them that they are to take home the family tree and with their parents try their best to fill in the chart completely.

Note: Students will be creating their own boxes and organization to their family tree. If there are any special family circumstances, be sure to reassure students that they can make any necessary changes.

Teacher Extension

- Ask students to bring pictures of their families. Scan the pictures into the computer and let your students add photos to their family tree slides.

Quick Steps

- Open a **Blank Presentation** in *PowerPoint* and select the **Organization Chart** slide.

- Double-click the **Organization Chart** and type your name where it says Type Title Here.

- Click on the boxes going down and type the names of your parents.

- Add more boxes going across or down by choosing from the tool bar above the screen.

- Add the number of boxes necessary until all the information about your family is displayed on the chart.

- Once the family tree is completely finished, pull down the **FILE** menu and select *Close*. Save information.

- Add pictures and titles to the slide.

- Save your slide with the file name (*Your name's family*).

- Print a copy of your slide.

Family Tree *(cont.)*

Procedure

Step 1   Open *PowerPoint* and select a **Blank Presentation**. Click **OK**.

Step 2   At the AutoLayout menu, select **Organization Chart**. Click **OK**.

Step 3   A slide template will appear on the screen. Double-click on the Organization Chart section of the slide.

Step 4   Click on the top box, highlight Type Name Here, and type your name. Delete the words Type Title Here.

Step 5   Click on the boxes going down and type the names of your parents. To delete boxes, click on the box and press **Delete** on the keyboard.

Step 6   You can add more boxes going across or down by choosing from the tool bar above the screen. Clicking on the **Co-worker** button will add a box going across the page for brothers and sisters. Clicking on **Subordinate** will add a box going down for grandparents.

Step 7   Continue adding information about your family until all the necessary boxes are filled.

Step 8   To change font and font color, pull down the **EDIT** menu and choose *Select All*. Then pull down the **TEXT** menu and make the font and font color changes you want on your family tree. To change the box color, pull down the **BOXES** menu, choose *Box Color*, and choose the color you want for your boxes.

Step 9   Once the family tree is completely finished, pull down the **FILE** menu, and *Close*. The computer will ask you if you want to update. Click **Yes**.

Step 10   The family tree will automatically be included on the *PowerPoint* slide. You can resize it by clicking on the black square handles and dragging the mouse.

Step 11   Move your mouse to the title bar at the top where it says "Click to add title" and give your family tree a name.

Step 12   Pull down the **INSERT** menu to add any pictures to your slide.

Step 13   Pull down the **FILE** menu and select *Save As*. Save the file as (*your name's family*).

Step 14   Pull down the **FILE** menu and select *Print*. Click on the Print button to print a hard copy of your slide. Click **OK** (PC) or **Print** (Mac).

Family Tree *(cont.)*

Student Planning Page

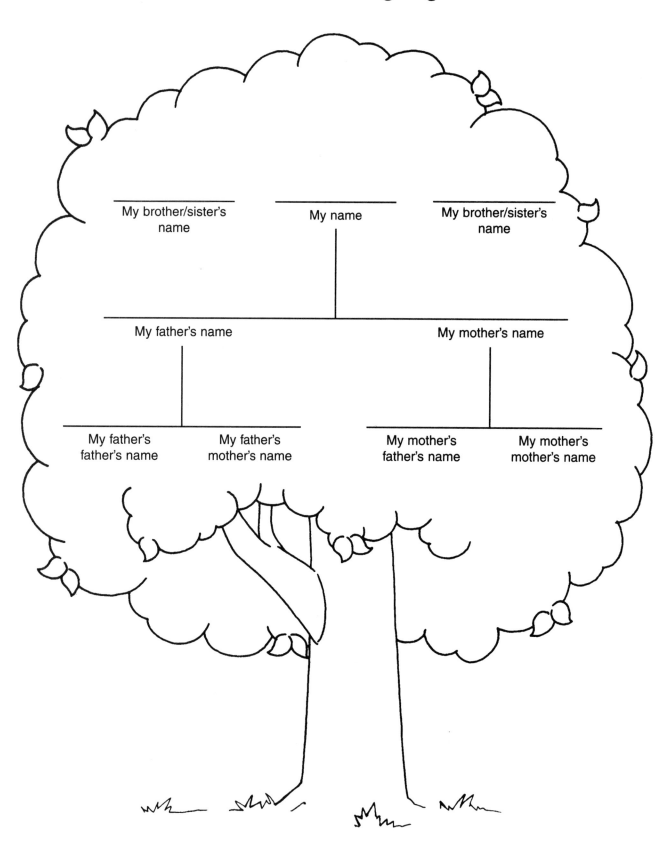

The American Government Structure

This Project

In this project, your students will research their national and local government representatives. They will take this information and place it into an Organizational Chart in a *PowerPoint* slide show.

Computer Skills

- Organizational Chart

Before Beginning

- Review with students the structure of the American government. Remind them that in our form of democratic government, the people are the ones who are most in charge of the country.

- Review the three branches of government (Legislative, Executive, and Judicial Branches) that all work together equally to help the country run smoothly.

- Tell students that they will be finding out who represents them in the various branches of the government.

- Have them complete the Student Planning Page on page 56 about who fills the offices in the national government. Students can complete the work sheet with teacher assistance, parent interviews, or Web searches. Some good sites for researching local and national representatives are:

    Contacting the Congress
    http://www.visi.com/juan/congress/

    White House for Kids
    http://www2.whitehouse.gov/WH/kids/html/home.html

    Oyez, Oyez, Oyez (Supreme Court)
    http://oyez.nwu.edu/

- Show students how to locate the template for this project.

The American Government Structure *(cont.)*

Quick Steps

- Open the (*Govern*) template.
- Double-click on the **Organization Chart**.
- Click on the People box at the top of the chart and enter your name where directed.
- Click on the President box and include the current president's name under the title.
- Click on the Vice President box and include the name of the current Vice President under the title.
- Choose the **Subordinate** icon and click on the Senate box. Add the name of one of the senators from your state.
- Choose the **Co-worker** icon and click on the name of your first senator. Add the name of the second senator from your state.
- Choose the **Subordinate** icon and click on the House of Representatives box. Add the name of the representative from your district.
- Choose the **Subordinate** icon and click on the Judicial Branch box. List the Chief Justice of the Supreme Court and the list the 8 other justices as Co-workers.
- Update the Organization Chart on the slide.
- Save your slide and print it.
- Fill in the subsequent slides with specific information about each branch of government.

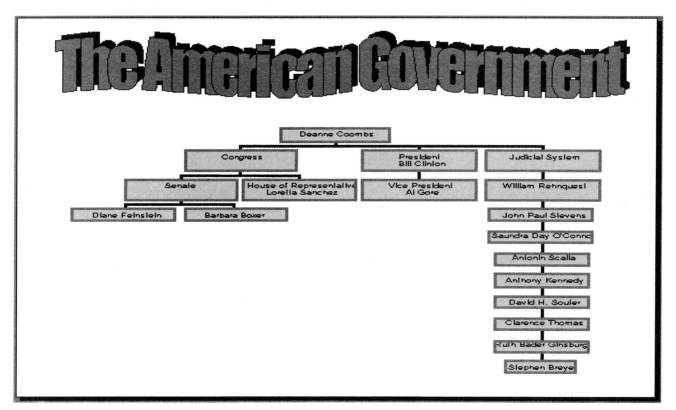

The American Government Structure *(cont.)*

Procedure

Step 1 Open *PowerPoint* and select **Open an existing presentation**. Click **OK**.

Step 2 Locate the (*Govern*) template and click **Open**.

Step 3 Move your mouse to the Organization Chart and double-click on the chart.

Step 4 Move your mouse over the People box at the top of the chart and click once.

Step 5 Move to the line where it asks for your name and type your name in the People box.

Step 6 Click your mouse outside the box to move to the next box.

Step 7 Move your mouse to the President box and click once.

Step 8 Type the name of the current President on the title line of the box.

Step 9 Click outside the box, then move your mouse to the Vice President box and click once.

Step 10 Type the name of the current Vice President on the title line of the box.

Step 11 Click outside the box.

Step 12 Select the **Subordinate** icon and click on the Senate box to make a box beneath the Senate.

Step 13 Select the **Co-worker** icon and click on the subordinate Senate box to make a box next to the subordinate box.

Step 14 Insert the names of the two senators from your state in the two boxes directly below the senate.

Step 15 Select the **Subordinate** icon and click on the House of Representatives box.

Step 16 Insert the name of your local district representative in this box.

Step 17 Select the **Subordinate** icon and click on the Judicial System box.

Step 18 Insert the name of the Supreme Court Chief Justice in this box.

Step 19 Using the **Subordinate** icon, insert eight subordinates to the Supreme Court Justice and add the names of all the justices of the court.

Step 20 In the Microsoft Organization Chart dialog box, pull down the **FILE** menu and select *Update Presentation* (PC) or *Update The American Government.ppt* (Mac).

Step 21 If you are working on a PC, pull down the **FILE** menu and select *Close*. If you are working on a Mac, pull down the **FILE** menu and select *Close and return to The American Government.ppt*.

Step 22 Pull down the **FILE** menu and select *Save As*. Give your file the name (*Government your initials*).

Step 23 Pull down the **FILE** menu and select *Print*. Click **OK** (PC) or **Print** (Mac).

Step 24 (Optional) On subsequent slides, fill in information and pictures that summarize each branches' members and their duties.

The American Government Structure *(cont.)*

Student Planning Page

Name: _____

President: _____

Vice-President: _____

Senator: _____

Senator: _____

House of Representative Member: _____

District Number: _____

Supreme Court Chief Justice: _____

Supreme Court Justices: _____

   1. _____

   2. _____

   3. _____

   4. _____

   5. _____

   6. _____

   7. _____

   8. _____

Touring the Solar System

This Project

In this project, your students will be creating a *PowerPoint* presentation about the planets of our solar system. They will add graphics of the sun and the planets along with textual information explaining some of the more important features of the planets.

Computer Skills

- Inserting graphics
- Finding and capturing graphics from the Internet
- Inserting text boxes
- Creating and demonstrating a *PowerPoint* Presentation

Before Beginning

- Review Internet Mini-Lesson on page 13–15.
- Some good solar system Web sites are:

    Star Child: A Learning Center for Young Astronomers
    http://starchild.gsfc.nasa.gov/docs/StarChild/StarChild.html

    The Nine Planets
    http://seds.lpl.arizona.edu/billa/trip

    Students for the Exploration and Development of Space
    http://www.seds.org/

    NASA Image eXchange
    http://nix.nasa.gov/nix.egi

- Have students complete the Student Planning Pages on pages 59-61.
- Show students how to locate the template for this project.

Quick Steps

- Open the (*Solar*) template.
- On the title slide, add a picture from the solar system. (Optional)
- Add a text box to add your name to the slide. Remember to change the font color to something other than black, because black won't show up on the black background.
- To create a slide about the sun:
    - Scroll to the next slide, with "sun" as its title.
    - Add a graphic of the sun. (Optional)
    - Add a text box to the bottom of the page with a short paragraph explaining any interesting facts you learned about the sun.
- Follow the above three steps to create slides about the nine planets in the solar system.
- Scroll to the last slide, Bibliography.
- On the bibliography page, add a text box to include any bibliographical information about the presentation. Be sure to cite web sites from which you borrowed graphics.
- Save and print your presentation.

Procedure

Step 1   Start *PowerPoint* program and select **Open an existing presentation**. Click **OK**. Select the (*Solar*) template from the CD and click **Open**.

Step 2   Pull down the **INSERT** menu, select *Picture*, and *From File*. Choose a picture of the solar system to add to your title slide. (One is provided on the CD-ROM in the folder named "Pictures.")

Step 3   Pull down the **VIEW** menu and select *Toolbars*. From the toolbar pop-up menu, be sure that the *Drawing* toolbar is selected.

Step 4   Pull down the **INSERT** menu and add a text box. An I-beam will appear on the screen. Place the text box where you want your name to be on the slide.

Step 5   Before you begin typing your name, go to the drawing toolbar on your screen. Move your mouse to the **Font Color** function on the toolbar. Click on the arrow to the right of the button and select a color other than black for your name.

Step 6   Type your name.

Step 7   Move your arrow to the right side of the screen to scroll down to the next slide.

Step 8   The next slide is about the Sun. Pull down the **INSERT** menu, select *Picture*, and *From File*. (A picture of the sun is provided on the CD-ROM in the folder named "Pictures.")

Step 9   Locate your picture from your files and click **Insert** to place it on your slide.

Step 10   Move your mouse to the boxes (handles) surrounding the graphic to click and drag your object to a proper location and size on your slide.

Step 11   Pull down the **INSERT** menu and select *Text Box*. An I-beam will appear on the screen. Place the text box where you want your short paragraph about the sun to be placed on the slide.

Step 12   Select the font color and type a short paragraph with the interesting information you have recorded on your Student Planning Pages on pages 59–61.

Step 13   Repeat steps 7 to 12 to create slides about Mercury, Venus, Earth, Mars, Saturn, Jupiter, Uranus, Neptune, and Pluto.

Step 14   Scroll to the final slide after Pluto, the Bibliography.

Step 15   Pull down the **INSERT** menu and select *Text Box*. An I-beam will appear on the screen. Place the text box on the page for your bibliographical information.

Step 16   Add any books and Web sites you used in your presentation to your Bibliography. Remember to cite the web cites or CD from which you captured your graphics.

Step 17   Pull down the **FILE** menu and select *Save As*. Give your file the name (*Solar your initials*).

Step 18   Pull down the **FILE** menu and select *Print*. Click **OK** (PC) or **Print** (Mac).

Touring the Solar System *(cont.)*

Student Planning Page

Name of Planet: **Mercury**

Diameter: _____

Distance from the Sun: _____

Number of Moons: _____

Fun Facts: _____

Sketch Mercury

Name of Planet: **Venus**

Diameter: _____

Distance from the Sun: _____

Number of Moons: _____

Fun Facts: _____

Sketch Venus

Name of Planet: **Earth**

Diameter: _____

Distance from the Sun: _____

Number of Moons: _____

Fun Facts: _____

Sketch Earth

Touring the Solar System *(cont.)*

Student Planning Page

Name of Planet: **Mars**

Diameter: _____

Distance from the Sun: _____

Number of Moons: _____

Fun Facts: _____

Sketch Mars

Name of Planet: **Saturn**

Diameter: _____

Distance from the Sun: _____

Number of Moons: _____

Fun Facts: _____

Sketch Saturn

Name of Planet: **Jupiter**

Diameter: _____

Distance from the Sun: _____

Number of Moons: _____

Fun Facts: _____

Sketch Jupiter

Touring the Solar System *(cont.)*

Student Planning Page

Name of Planet: **Uranus**

Diameter: _____

Distance from the Sun: _____

Number of Moons: _____

Fun Facts: _____

Sketch Uranus

Name of Planet: **Neptune**

Diameter: _____

Distance from the Sun: _____

Number of Moons: _____

Fun Facts: _____

Sketch Neptune

Name of Planet: **Pluto**

Diameter: _____

Distance from the Sun: _____

Number of Moons: _____

Fun Facts: _____

Sketch Pluto

Nutrition

This Project

In this project, your students will use a slide show format to document the types of foods they eat and to demonstrate whether they are meeting their basic daily nutritional requirements.

Computer Skills

- Adding graphics
- Adding text boxes
- Using and adding bullets
- Creating a complete slide show presentation

Before Beginning

- Review the Food Pyramid on page 65 with your students.
- Review portions and servings with your students.
- Have students use the Student Planning Pages on pages 66–67 to record the food they eat in a single day.
- Show students how to locate the template for this project.

Quick Steps

- Open the (*Pyramid*) template.
- Insert a text box listing all the foods you ate at breakfast.
- Insert graphics of some of the foods you ate at breakfast.
- Scroll to the next slide, Lunch.
- Insert a text box listing all the foods you ate at lunch.
- Insert graphics of some of the foods you ate at lunch.
- Scroll to the next slide, Dinner.
- Insert a text box listing all the foods that you ate at dinner.
- Insert graphics of some of the foods you ate at dinner.
- Scroll to the next slide, Snacks.
- Insert a text box listing all the snacks you ate throughout the day.
- Insert graphics of some of the snacks you ate.
- Scroll down the next slide, My Nutrition.
- Click on the text box that asks for the number of servings you ate in each category.
- Fill in the number of servings that you ate for all of the categories.
- Click on the question at the bottom of the page.
- Answer whether or not you ate foods that match the nutritional requirements on the food pyramid.
- Resize the text boxes as needed.
- Save and print.

Procedure

Step 1   Open *PowerPoint* and select **Open an existing presentation**. Click **OK**. Select the (*Pyramid*) template from the CD-ROM and click **Open**.

Step 2   The first slide of the presentation is Breakfast. Pull down the **INSERT** menu and select *Text Box*.

Step 3   Move your mouse to place the arrow where you want the text box to be on your slide.

Step 4   Click the Bullets icon to make a list of all the foods you ate at breakfast.

Step 5   Pull down the **INSERT** menu and select *Picture*.

Step 6   Select *Clip Art*. Select a type of food you want to put on your slide and click **Insert**.

Step 7   Select the graphic and grab one of the handles with the mouse to resize as needed.

Step 8   Move your mouse to the scroll bar at the right of the screen and scroll down to the next slide, Lunch.

Step 9   Pull down the **INSERT** menu and select *Text Box*.

Step 10   Move your mouse to place the arrow where you want your text box to be on your slide.

Step 11   Click the **Bullets** icon to make a list of all the foods you ate at lunch.

Step 12   Pull down the **INSERT** menu and select *Picture*.

Step 13   Select *Clip Art*. Select a type of food you want to put on your slide and click **Insert**.

Step 14   Select the graphic and grab one of the handles with the mouse to resize as needed.

Step 15   Move your mouse to the scroll bar at the right of the screen and scroll down to the next slide, Dinner.

Step 16   Pull down the **INSERT** menu and select *Text Box*.

Step 17   Move your mouse to place the arrow where you want your text box to be on your slide.

Step 18   Click the **Bullets** icon to make a list of all the foods you ate at dinner.

Step 19   Pull down the **INSERT** menu and select *Picture*.

Step 20   Select *Clip Art*. Select a type of food you want to put on your slide and click **Insert**.

Step 21   Select the graphic and grab one of the handles with the mouse to resize as needed.

Step 22   Move your mouse to the scroll bar at the right of the screen and scroll down to the next slide, Snacks.

Step 23   Pull down the **INSERT** menu and select *Text Box*.

Step 24   Move your mouse to place the arrow where you want your text box to be on your slide.

Step 25   Click the **Bullets** icon to make a list of all of the snack foods that you ate throughout the entire day. Be sure to include snacks that you ate between breakfast and lunch, lunch and dinner, and dinner and bedtime.

Step 26 Pull down the **INSERT** menu, select *Picture* and then *Clip Art*.

Step 27 Locate clip art for snack food you ate that day and click **Insert** to add to your slide.

Step 28 Move your mouse to the scroll bar at the right of the screen and scroll down to the next slide, My Nutrition.

Step 29 Move your mouse over the number of servings of each of the food groups and click once to access the text box.

Step 30 Add up the number of servings you ate in a single day of each of the food groups and enter them into the text box.

Step 31 Move your mouse over the questions at the bottom of the page and click once to access the text box.

Step 32 Answer the questions in the text box.

Step 33 Use the handles to resize the text boxes as needed.

Step 34 Pull down the **FILE** menu and select *Save As*. Give your file the name (Nutrition your initials).

Step 35 Pull down the **FILE** menu and select *Print*. Click **OK** (PC) or **Print** (Mac).

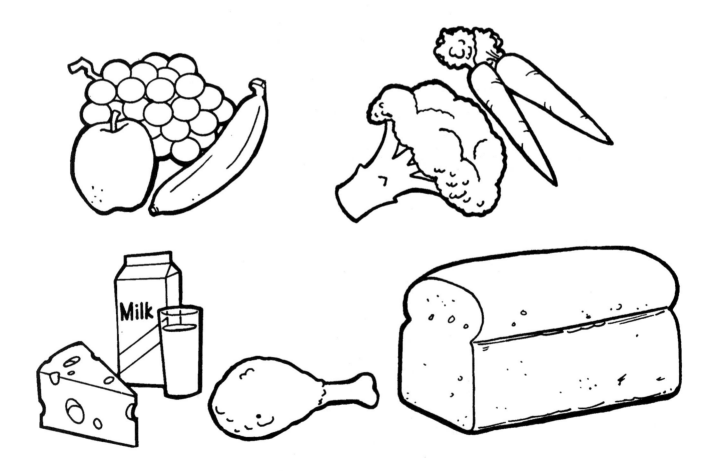

Nutrition

Food Pyramid

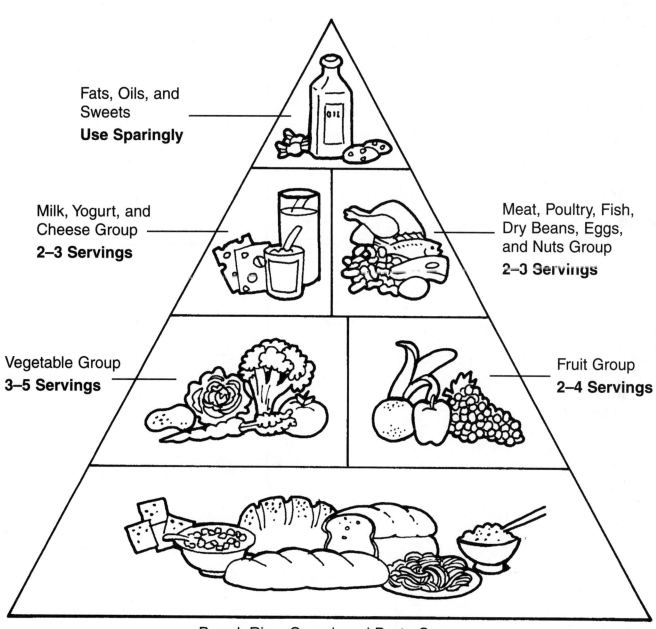

Fats, Oils, and Sweets
Use Sparingly

Milk, Yogurt, and Cheese Group
2–3 Servings

Meat, Poultry, Fish, Dry Beans, Eggs, and Nuts Group
2–3 Servings

Vegetable Group
3–5 Servings

Fruit Group
2–4 Servings

Bread, Rice, Cereal, and Pasta Group
6–11 Servings

Nutrition *(cont.)*

Student Planning Page

Today you are going to keep track of everything you eat. You need to record all the food you eat at breakfast, lunch, and dinner. You also need to write down all the snacks and treats you eat throughout the day. Under each category, list the food you ate beside the food group it belongs to.

Name: _____

Food Groups	Breakfast	Lunch	Dinner	Snack
Bread:				
Fruits:				
Vegetables:				
Dairy:				
Meat:				
Fats/Sugars:				

Nutrition *(cont.)*

Student Planning Page

Use your food record to complete the graph below.

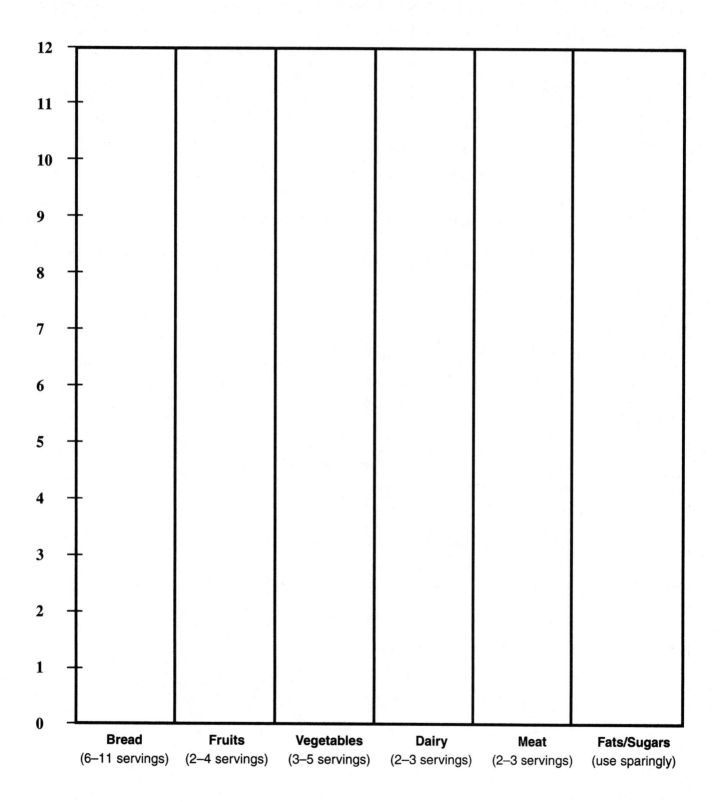

Discovering Matter

This Project

In this project, your students will explore the three phases of matter. They will create slides with illustrations and definitions for each phase.

Computer Skills

- Inserting graphics
- Inserting text boxes

Before Beginning

- Review with students the three phases of matter: solid, liquid, and gas.
- On the board, create a list of things that are solids, liquids, and gases so students are familiar with tangible examples of the three phases.
- Remind them that all phases of matter have two things in common: they have weight and they take up space.
- Show students how to locate the template for this project.
- Have students complete the Student Planning Page on page 70.

Quick Steps

- Open the *PowerPoint* template called (*Matter*).
- Add graphics of the three different phases of matter to the title slide.
- Add a text box with your name to the title slide.
- Scroll down to the next slide, Solid.
- Add a graphic or graphics of some solid objects to the clip art box.
- Use the text box to add a definition of a solid.
- Scroll down to the next slide, Liquid.
- Add a graphic or graphics of some liquids to the clip art box.
- Use the text box to add a definition of a liquid.
- Scroll down to the next slide, Gases.
- Add a graphic of graphics of some gases to the clip art box.
- Use the text box to add a definition of a gas.
- Save and print.

Discovering Matter *(cont.)*

Procedure

Step 1   Open *PowerPoint* and select **Open an existing presentation**. Click **OK**.

Step 2   Locate the (*Matter*) template and click **Open**.

Step 3   Pull down the **INSERT** menu, select *Picture*, and *Clip Art*. Scroll through the available clip art and select a picture of a solid. Click **Insert**.

Step 4   Repeat Step 3 and insert pictures of liquids and gases on your title slide.

Step 5   Pull down the **INSERT** menu and select *Text Box*.

Step 6   Move the I-beam on your screen to where you want to place your text box and click once.

Step 7   Type your name in the text box.

Step 8   Use your mouse and the handles to resize and move the graphics and text boxes until you have a nice layout.

Step 9   Move your mouse to the right side of the screen to scroll down to the next slide, Solids.

Step 10   Move your mouse to the Clip Art box and double-click. Scroll through the graphics to locate the graphic of a solid. Select the graphic with your mouse and click Insert.

Step 11   Move your mouse to the text box and click once. Type your definition of a solid in the text box.

Step 12   Move your mouse to the right side of the screen to scroll down to the next slide, Liquids.

Step 13   Move your mouse to the Clip Art box and double-click. Scroll through the graphics to locate a graphic of a liquid. Select the graphic with your mouse and click Insert.

Step 14   Move your mouse to the text box and click once. Type your definition of a liquid in the text box.

Step 15   Move your mouse to the right hand side of the screen to scroll down to the next slide, Gases.

Step 16   Move your mouse to the Clip Art box and double-click. Scroll through the graphics to locate a graphic of a gas. Select the graphic with your mouse and click **Insert**.

Step 17   Move your mouse to the text box and click once. Type your definition of a gas in the text box.

Step 18   Pull down the **FILE** menu and select *Save As*. Give your file the name (*Matter your initials*).

Step 19   Pull down the **FILE** menu and select *Print*. Click **OK** (PC) or **Print** (Mac).

Discovering Matter *(cont.)*

Student Planning Page

A **solid** is: _____

List some examples of solids.

1. _____
2. _____
3. _____
4. _____
5. _____

A **liquid** is: _____

List some examples of liquids.

1. _____
2. _____
3. _____
4. _____
5. _____

A **gas** is: _____

List some examples of a gas.

1. _____
2. _____
3. _____
4. _____
5. _____

What are the two things that all types of matter have in common?

1. _____
2. _____

Animal Report

This Project

In this project, your students will create a *PowerPoint* presentation to demonstrate their knowledge about the adaptations of an animal. They will report on this animal's habitat, its predators and prey, and its adaptations to its environment.

Computer Skills

- Adding graphics
- Adding text boxes

Before Beginning

- Complete the Internet Mini-Lesson on pages 13–15.

- Have each student select an animal to research. A good thing to do is to list some animals that have a lot of research available and make this list available to your students. They can also draw the names of their animals out of a hat. Use the animal list on page 77.

- Below is a list of some good Web sites for your students to use to research their animals:

    Yahooligans
    http://www.yahooligans.com

    SeaWorld/Busch Gardens Animal Information Database
    http://www.seaworld.org/

    Electronic Zoo
    http://netvet.wustl.edu/e-zoo.htm

- Review adaptive behaviors. For instance, a bee uses a "stinger" to protect itself from predators.

- Have students complete the Student Planning Pages on pages 75–76.

- Show them how to locate the template for this project.

Quick Steps

- Open *PowerPoint* and select the *(Animal)* template.

- Insert a graphic of your selected animal from your files.

- Add your name to the text box at the bottom of the slide.

- Change the WordArt title to your animal's name.

- Scroll down to the next slide, Habitat.

- Insert a graphic from your files of your animal in its natural habitat.

- Add a text box describing your animal's habitat.

- Scroll down to the next slide, Predators.

- Insert a graphic or graphics of some of your animal's predators.

- Add a text box listing your animal's predators and explaining how dangerous they are to its existence.

- Scroll down to the next slide, Prey.

- Insert a graphic or graphics of the food or prey your animal eats.

- Add a text box listing the types of food your animal consumes and explaining why your animal eats those types of food.

- Scroll down to the next slide, Adaptations.

- Insert a graphic showing either your animal's adaptive behavior or its adaptive body part(s).

- Add a text box explaining how your animal has adapted to its habitat.

- Scroll down to the next slide, Bibliography.

- Click on the text box on the screen. Add all the bibliographical information for the resources used in this report. Be sure to include the Web sites where you captured graphics.

- Save and print.

Procedure

Step 1   Open *PowerPoint* and select **Open an existing presentation**. Click **OK**.

Step 2   Locate the (*Animal*) template and click **Open**.

Step 3   Pull down the **INSERT** menu, select *Picture*, and *From File*. Locate your title slide picture of your animal. Select the file with your mouse and click **Insert**.

Step 4   Move your mouse over the My Animal title at the top of the page and double-click.

Step 5   Remove the text in the pop-up box by highlighting and deleting. Add the name of your animal to the title. Click **OK**.

Step 6   Move your mouse to the bottom of the slide and click once where it says Name.

Step 7   Type your name in the text box.

Step 8   Use your mouse and the handles to resize the text boxes and graphics as needed on your title slide.

Step 9   Move your mouse to the right side of the page and use the scroll bar to scroll to the next slide, Habitat.

Step 10   Pull down the **INSERT** menu, select *Picture*, and *From File*. Locate a picture of your animal in its natural habitat. Select the file with your mouse and click **Insert**.

Step 11   Pull down the **INSERT** menu and select *Text Box*.

Step 12   An I-beam will appear on the slide. Click once where you want to place the text box.

Step 13   In the text box, type a paragraph describing your animal's habitat. Use the Student Planning Pages as a guide.

Step 14   Use the mouse and handles to resize your graphic and text box as needed.

Step 15   Move your mouse to the right side of the screen and use the scroll bar to scroll to your next slide, Predators.

Step 16   Pull down the **INSERT** menu, select *Picture*, and *From File*. Locate a graphic of one of your animal's predators, select it with your mouse and click **Insert**.

Step 17   Repeat Step 16 for all the graphics that you want to place on your slide.

Step 18   Pull down the **INSERT** menu and select *Text Box*.

Step 19   List your animal's predators in the text box. Write a few sentences describing how your animal defends itself against its predators.

Step 20   Move your mouse to the right hand side of the screen and use the scroll bar to scroll down to the next slide, Prey.

Step 21   Pull down the **INSERT** menu, select *Picture*, and *From File*. Locate a graphic of the prey your animal eats, select it with your mouse and click **Insert**.

Step 22   Repeat Step 21 for all the graphics you want to place on your slide.

Step 23   Pull down the **INSERT** menu and select *Text Box*.

Step 24 In the text box, list the prey and types of food your animal eats. In a couple of sentences, explain how your animal captures or finds its food.

Step 25 Move your mouse to the right side of the screen and use the scroll bar to scroll down to the next slide, Adaptations.

Step 26 Pull down the **INSERT** menu, select *Picture*, and *From File*. Locate a picture showing your animal in its natural habitat or one of its adaptive body parts. Select the picture with your mouse and click Insert.

Step 27 Pull down the **INSERT** menu and select *Text Box*.

Step 28 In the text box, type a paragraph about your animal's adaptive behaviors. Explain what would happen to your animal if it were taken out of its natural habitat.

Step 29 Move your mouse to the right side of the screen and use the scroll bar to scroll down to the next slide, Bibliography.

Step 30 Use your mouse to click once on the text box. Type in the bibliographical information for the book and Internet resources you used to research your presentation.

Step 31 Pull down the **FILE** menu and select *Save As*. Give your file the name (*animal your initials*).

Step 32 Pull down the **FILE** menu and select *Print*. Click **OK** (PC) or **Print** (Mac).

Animal Report *(cont.)*

Student Planning Page: Habitat and Predators

You are going to be creating a *PowerPoint* presentation on your animal. Research your animal and fill out the information below. Use it as a guide in creating your presentation.

Name: _____

Your animal's name: _____

Draw a picture of your animal in its natural habitat.

_____

In a couple of sentences, describe your animal's habitat. _____

_____

_____

_____

What are your animal's predators? _____

_____

_____

_____

Does your animal have any defenses against its predators?_____

_____

_____

_____

Animal Report *(cont.)*

Student Planning Page: Prey and Adaptation

What types of plants or animals does your animal eat?

_____

_____

_____

How does your animal find food? Does it have any natural systems to help it locate food?

_____

_____

_____

Does your animal have any special body parts it uses to eat, hunt, or build a home?

_____

_____

_____

What do you think would happen to your animal if it were taken from its habitat and moved to another one?

_____

_____

_____

Would it survive? Why or why not?

_____

_____

_____

Animal Report *(cont.)*

Teacher Planning Page

Copy this page and cut out the animal names for your students to draw out of a hat. This list is comprised of animals on which a lot of information is available. There are some blank lines for you to add your own animals.

lion	toad	deer
shark	turtle	rattlesnake
bee	bald eagle	jellyfish
cobra	penguin	porcupine
dolphin	tiger	killer whale
blue whale	elephant	coyote
crocodile	rhino	lizard
alligator	hippo	wolf
frog		

Our Favorite Cookies

This Project

In this project, your students will record data, input it into a spreadsheet, and create graphs. The topic that they will be working on will be one of their favorites—food! This activity uses cookies, but you can easily adapt it to be a seasonal activity by using holiday foods.

Computer Skills

- Building a Spreadsheet
- Data Entry
- Creating a graph

Before Beginning

- Review with your students how to gather and record data.
- Have each student or group complete the data on the Student Planning Page on page 80. They will be conducting a survey of students in your classroom or in another classroom at the school.
- Show students how to locate the template for this project.

Quick Steps

- Open the *PowerPoint* template called (*Cookies*).
- Click on the graph area to enter the data.
- Move across each row to input the number of students that like each kind of cookie best.
- Close the pop-up spreadsheet.
- Using the **FORMAT** menu, make any desired color or font changes to the graph.
- Save your slide with the file name (*Your name's cookies*).
- Print a copy of your slide.

Our Favorite Cookies *(cont.)*

Procedure

Step 1 Open *PowerPoint* and select **Open an Existing Presentation**. Click **OK**.

Step 2 A pop-up box with all the files will appear on the screen. Select (*Cookies*) and click **Open**.

Step 3 Move the mouse over the blank graph on the slide. Then right-click your mouse if you are using a PC. Double-click your mouse if you are using a Mac.

Step 4 Click on cell A1 and enter the number of girls who said chocolate chip cookies were their favorite.

Step 5 Use the tab key or arrow key to move to the box on the right, B1. Input the number of girls who chose peanut butter cookies as their favorite.

Step 6 Move to the next box, C1. Input the number of girls who chose sugar cookies as their favorite.

Step 7 Move to the next box, D1. Input the number of girls who chose oatmeal cookies as their favorite.

Step 8 Move to the next box, E1. Input the number of girls who chose a type of cookie not listed in the survey as their favorite.

Step 9 Click in cell A2. Input the number of boys who chose chocolate chip cookies as their favorite.

Step 10 Use the tab key to move along the rest of line 2. Input the numbers from your survey about the boys into the appropriate cells.

Step 11 Click in cell A3. Input the total number of girls and boys who chose chocolate chip cookies as their favorite.

Step 12 Use the tab key to move along the rest of line 3. Input the numbers from your survey about boys and girls into the appropriate cells.

Step 13 If you are using a PC, close the pop-up spreadsheet by clicking on the "x" in the upper left-hand corner of the box. On a Mac, go to the **FILE** menu and select *Quit and Return to Favorite Cookies.ppt*.

Step 14 If you are using a PC, double-click on the graph you have just created. You will see a menu where you can change the border or the background color of your graph. On a Mac, double-click on the graph, then go to the **Graph in Favorite Cookies.ppt-Chart** pop-up menu. Double-click on the graph again and you will be able to change the border or background color of your graph.

Step 15 Once you have chosen a new color or border for your graph, click **OK**.

Step 16 Pull down the **FILE** menu and select *Save As*. Change the file name to (*your initials Favorite Cookies*).

Step 17 Pull down the **FILE** menu and select *Print*. Click on the Print button to print a hard copy of your graph. Click **OK** (PC) or **Print** (Mac).

Our Favorite Cookies *(cont.)*

Student Planning Page

You will be conducting a survey of all the students in your class. You will need to ask each student to tell you his or her favorite kind of cookie. As you ask each student, you will put a tally mark under the type of cookie they like best. There is a row for girls, boys, and girls and boys combined. When you take the survey, just tally in the "girls" row and the "boys" row. You can add the two numbers at the end to complete the girls and boys row.

Class Survey

	Chocolate Chip	Peanut Butter	Sugar	Oatmeal	Other
Girls					
Boys					
Girls and Boys					

Geometric Shapes

This Project

In this project, your students will create a slide show using *PowerPoint*'s AutoShape tool to demonstrate different types of geometric shapes. Students will illustrate a circle, triangle, and rectangle and write a definition for each geometric shape.

Computer Skills

- Using text boxes
- Adding and using the auto shape function
- Importing graphics

Before Beginning

- Review with students some geometric shapes: circle, triangle, and rectangle.
- Make a list on the board of where we find these shapes in the real world.

  Circle: Earth, basketball hoops, sun, coins, etc.
  Triangle: Pyramids, cheerleader pyramids, Mt. Fuji etc.
  Rectangle: handball courts, videocassettes, windows, doors, etc.

- Review the Internet Mini-Lesson on pages 13-15 for students to find real-world examples of geometric shapes. A good web site for geometric definitions is:

  Harcourt Brace Math Glossary
  http://www.hbschool.com/glossary/math/

- Show students how to locate the template for this project.

Teacher Extension

- Add a new slide for any other geometric shapes your students have been studying. Do this by opening the Geometric Shapes template, pulling down the **INSERT** menu and selecting *New Slide*.

Quick Steps

- Open *PowerPoint* template called (*Shapes*).
- Click on the definition text box and write your own definition for a circle.
- Use the **AutoShape** tool to draw some different size, shape, and color circles.
- Insert clip art of things you find in the real world that are circles.
- Move to the next slide, Triangles.
- Click on the definition text box and write your own definition for a triangle.
- Use the **AutoShape** tool to draw some different size, shape, and color triangles.
- Insert clip art of things you find in the real world that are triangles.
- Move to the next slide, Rectangles.
- Click on the definition text box and write your own definition for a rectangle.
- Use the **AutoShape** tool to draw some different size, shape, and color triangles.
- Insert clip art of things you find in the real word that are rectangles.
- Print and save your work.

Geometric Shapes *(cont.)*

Procedure

Step 1   Open *PowerPoint*, select **Open an existing presentation** and click **OK**. Locate the (*Shapes*) template and click **Open**.

Step 2   The first slide will be about Circles. Move your mouse over the text box where it asks you to write a definition and click once.

Step 3   Highlight the text in the box and delete it. Type your own definition of a circle in the text box.

Step 4   Pull down the **VIEW** menu and select *Toolbars*. Make sure that the *Drawing* toolbar is selected.

Step 5   Move your mouse to the **AutoShapes** button and click. Move to the *Basic Shapes* menu and select an oval.

Step 6   A crosshair will appear on your screen. Keeping the **Shift** key down, click and drag your arrow to make a circle you like on your slide.

Step 7   Release your mouse button. Pull down the **FORMAT** menu and select *Colors and Lines*. Change the Fill and Line color. Click **OK**.

Step 8   Repeat steps 5-7 until you have the number of desired circles of different sizes, shapes, and colors on your slide.

Step 9   Pull down the **INSERT** menu, select *Picture*, and choose either *Clip Art* or *From File*. Locate a "real world" picture of a circle and click **Insert**.

Step 10   Use the handles on the graphic to resize and place the graphic on your slide.

Step 11   Move your mouse to the scroll bar on the right side of your screen and scroll down to the next slide, Triangle.

Step 12   Move your mouse over the text box where it asks you to write a definition and click once.

Step 13   Highlight the text in the box and delete it. Type your own definition of a triangle in the text box.

Step 14   Move your mouse to the **AutoShapes** button and click. Move to the *Basic Shapes* menu and select a triangle.

Step 15   An arrow will appear on your screen. Click and drag your arrow to make a triangle you like on your slide. Release your mouse button.

Step 16   Pull down the **FORMAT** menu and select *Colors and Lines*. Change the Fill and Line color. Click **OK**.

Step 17   Repeat steps 14-16 until you have the number of desired triangles of different sizes, shapes, and colors on your slide.

Step 18   Pull down the **INSERT** menu, select *Picture*, and choose either *Clip Art* or *From File*. Locate a "real world" picture of a triangle and click **Insert**.

Step 19   Use the handles on the graphic to resize and place the graphic on your slide.

Step 20   Move your mouse to the scroll bar on the right hand side of your screen and scroll down to the next slide, Rectangle.

Step 21   Move your mouse over the text box where it asks you to write a definition and click on your mouse once.

Step 22   Highlight the text in the box and delete it. Type your own definition of a rectangle in the text box.

Step 23   Move your mouse to the **AutoShapes** button and click. Move to the ***Basic Shapes*** menu and select a rectangle.

Step 24   An arrow will appear on your screen. Click and drag your arrow to make a rectangle on your slide. Release your mouse button.

Step 25   Pull down the **FORMAT** menu and select ***Colors and Lines***. Change the Fill and Line color. Click **OK**.

Step 26   Repeat steps 23-25 until you have the number of desired rectangles of different sizes, shapes, and colors on your slide.

Step 27   Pull down the **INSERT** menu, select ***Picture***, and choose either ***Clip Art*** or ***From File***. Locate a real-world picture of a rectangle and click Insert.

Step 28   Use the handles on the graphic to resize and place the graphic on your slide.

Step 29   If you used any graphics from a web site, pull down the **INSERT** menu and select ***New Slide***. Pull down the **INSERT** menu, select ***Text Box*** and type a bibliography of all the Web sites you used.

Step 30   Pull down the **FILE** menu and select ***Save As***. Give your file the name (*Geometry your initials*).

Step 31   Pull down the **FILE** menu and select ***Print***. Click **OK** (PC) or **Print** (Mac).

A closed figure where all points on the figure are the same distance from the center point.

Math with Candies

This Project

In this project, your students will predict the number of each color of candies they find in a package of multicolored candy. They will record their results and then collect data on the actual number of each candy color. They will graph these results on a *PowerPoint* slide.

Computer Skills

- Using spreadsheets in *PowerPoint*
- Creating graphs in *PowerPoint*

Before Beginning

- Review with your students how to read and create bar graphs.
- Explain that they are going to predict the number of each color of candy in their package before opening it. Tell them they need to record their predictions on the Student Planning Page on page 86.
- This project can be completed individually, in pairs, or in small groups.
- Show students how to locate the template for this project.

Quick Steps

- Open *PowerPoint* and select the (*Math*) template.
- Add a title to the slide.
- Change the background color of the slide.
- Double-click to access the spreadsheet.
- Enter the predicted data on Line 1.
- Enter the actual data on Line 2.
- Click back on the main screen to see the graph.
- Change the background colors of the bar graph.
- Save and print.

Math with Candies *(cont.)*

Procedure

Step 1   Open *PowerPoint* and select **Open an existing presentation**. Click **OK**.

Step 2   Locate the *(Math)* template and click **Open**.

Step 3   Move the mouse over "Click to add title." Click once and type a title for your graph.

Step 4   If you are using a PC, move your mouse over the graph and double-click to access the datasheet. If you are using a Mac, click on the chart, then select *Edit*, *Chart Object* and ***Open***.

Step 5   On the PC, a datasheet will appear on the screen. On the Mac, both a datasheet and a chart will appear: click on the datasheet. Move your mouse to cell A1, click on it and enter your prediction for Red.

Step 6   Use the arrow keys to move to cell B1. Enter your prediction for Orange.

Step 7   Repeat Step 6 to enter all your predictions in Line 1.

Step 8   Use the arrow keys to move to cell A2. Enter the actual amount of red candies you found in your package.

Step 9   Move to cell B2. Enter the actual amount of orange candies you found in your package.

Step 10   Repeat Step 9 for all the colors you actually found in your package of candy.

Step 11   On the PC, move your mouse back to the original slide and click to update the graph. To close the datasheet, click the X in its upper right hand corner. On the Mac, Choose **FILE** and select ***Quit and Return to Math with Candies.ppt***.

Step 12   Pull down the **FORMAT** menu and select *Background*. From the **Background Fill** pop-up menu, pull down the arrow and select **More Colors**.

Step 13   A honeycomb of colors will appear. Use your mouse to select a color and click **OK**. Click **Apply to All**.

Step 14   Click on the graph. Pull down the **FORMAT** menu and select *Object*. From this pop-up window, you can change the background color of your graph and of the lines on the graph.

Step 15   Pull down the **FILE** menu and select *Save As*. Give your file the name (*Candies your initials*).

Step 16   Pull down the **FILE** menu and select *Print*. Click **OK** (PC) or **Print** (Mac).

Math with Candies *(cont.)*

Student Planning Page

Prediction

Take a look at a bag of multicolored candies and predict how many of each color you think you will find in the bag. Record your predictions below.

	Predictions
Red	
Orange	
Green	
Yellow	
Purple	

Actual

Open your bag of candies and separate them into piles by color. Count the number of each color and record the actual below.

	Predictions
Red	
Orange	
Green	
Yellow	
Purple	

Have fun eating your candies!

My Famous Artist

This Project

In this project, your students will research an artist in the library and on the Internet. The students will practice capturing graphics from the Internet and importing them into a *PowerPoint* presentation. They will learn to organize all their information into a report format in *PowerPoint* and present it clearly and concisely. If time permits, allow your students to demonstrate their presentation to the entire class or give them free time to explore their friends' presentations.

Computer Skills

- Word Processing

- Capturing graphics from the Internet

- Inserting graphics into a *PowerPoint* presentation

- Formatting and presenting information

- Changing background colors

Before Beginning

- Help students choose an artist for their report. Give them a list of well-known artists from which to choose.

- Use the Internet Mini-lesson on pages 13–15 with your students to familiarize your students with capturing graphics off the Web.

- Remind them that any graphics or information they use from the Internet must be cited in their bibliography.

- Have them complete the Student Planning Pages on pages 91-92 to help gather the information for their presentation.

- Some good Web sites containing information on artists are:

    World Wide Web Virtual Library: Museums
    http://www.icom.org/vlmp/
    This site has all the museums listed here. Search the name of your artist.

    National Museum of American Art
    http://www.nmaa.si.edu/
    If you have chosen an American artist, search for your artist here.

    IPL Youth Division
    http://www.ipl.org/youth/
    This is a good library of information for everything. Have students search the name of their artist.

    Yahooligans
    http://www.yahooligans.com/
    Yahooligans contains lots of information for students. Have students search the name of their artist.

My Famous Artist *(cont.)*

Quick Steps

- Open a new *PowerPoint* Blank Presentation. Click **OK**.

- Select the Title slide and enter your artist's name and birth/death dates.

- Pull down the **FORMAT** menu and select *Slide Color Scheme* to change the background color of your presentation.

- Insert a picture of your artist onto the title slide.

- Open a new slide and select the **Text and Clip Art Slide**. Choose a piece of artwork by your artist. Insert the name of this piece in the title. Then insert a graphic of the piece in the clip art section. Include anything you have learned about that piece in the text box.

- Open a new slide and select the **Text and Clip Art Slide**. Choose another piece of artwork by your artist. Insert the name of the piece in the title and a graphic of the piece in the clip art section. Include anything you have learned about that piece in the text box.

- Open a new slide and select **Bulleted List**. Insert the name of your artist at the top. In the bulleted list section, write any interesting facts you learned about your artist's life.

- Open a new slide and select the **Title only** slide. Create a bibliography on this slide. Insert a text box for the bibliography on the bottom of the slide.

- Save and print your work.

My Famous Artist *(cont.)*

Procedure

Step 1   Open a new *PowerPoint* **Blank Presentation**. Click **OK**.

Step 2   From the AutoLayout Menu, select **Title Slide**. Click **OK**.

Step 3   Move the mouse to "Click to add title." Click and type the name of your artist.

Step 4   Move the mouse to "Click to add subtitle." Click and type the years your artist was alive.

Step 5   Pull down the **FORMAT** menu and select *Slide Color Scheme*. Select **Custom** and **Change Color**. A honeycomb of colors will appear. Choose a background color that you would like throughout your slide show. Click **OK** and then click **Apply to All**.

Step 6   Pull down the **INSERT** menu, select *Picture*, and *From File*. Locate a picture of your artist if available from your files and insert onto the slide.

Step 7   Pull down the **INSERT** menu and select *New Slide*. From the **AutoLayout** menu select the **Text and Clip Art** slide. Click **OK**.

Step 8   Move the mouse to Click to add title. Add the title of the piece of artwork you will be showing on the slide.

Step 9   Move the mouse to Double-click to add clip art. Select **Import Clip(s)** and locate your picture of the artist's artwork in your files. Import into the clip art graphic and insert it into your document.

Step 10   Move the mouse to Click to add text. This will be a bulleted place for you to add any facts you know about the piece of art work to the slide.

Step 11   Pull down the **INSERT** menu and select *New Slide*. From the **AutoLayout** menu, select the **Text and Clip Art** slide. Click **OK**.

Step 12   Move the mouse to Click to add title. Add the title of the piece of artwork you will be showing on the slide.

Step 13   Move the mouse to Double-click to add clip art. Select **Import Clip(s)** and locate your picture of the artist's artwork in your files. Import into clip art and insert into your document.

Step 14   Move the mouse to Click to add text. This will be a bulleted place for you to add facts any facts you know about the piece of art work to the slide.

Step 15   Pull down the **INSERT** menu and select *New Slide*. From the **AutoLayout** menu, select the **Bulleted List**. Click **OK**.

Step 16   Move the mouse to Click to add title and write your artist's name and the word "life."

Step 17   Move the mouse to Click to add text. A bulleted list will appear. In this text box, include any interesting facts you have learned about your artist.

Step 19   Pull down the **INSERT** menu and select *New Slide*. From the **AutoLayout** menu select the **Title Only** slide. Click **OK**.

Step 20   Move the mouse to Click to add title. Write "Bibliography" for the title of this slide.

Step 21   Pull down the **INSERT** menu and select *Text Box*. An arrow will appear for you to draw a text box. Click on the screen to add a text box.

Step 22 List a bibliography of all the books, web sites and periodicals you used for your information and artwork.

Step 23 Pull down the **FILE** menu and select *Save As*. Give your file the name (*your artist's name your initials*). Click **OK**.

Step 24 Practice using your presentation as a slide show.

Step 25 Pull down the **FILE** menu and select *Print*. Click **OK** (PC) or **Print** (Mac).

My Famous Artist *(cont.)*

Student Planning Page

Name: _____

Artist's Name: _____

Artist's Birth: _____

Artist's Death (if deceased): _____

Why did you choose this person as your artist? _____

_____

Where did your artist live? _____

_____

What type of artwork did your artist do? _____

_____

Why is your artist famous? _____

_____

Was he/she famous while he/she was alive? _____

_____

List any fun facts you learned about your artist. _____

_____

_____

_____

_____

My Famous Artist *(cont.)*

Student Planning Page

Name of a piece of artwork your artist created. _____

When did your artist make this piece of artwork? _____

Where is this piece of artwork now? _____

Do you like this piece of artwork? Why or why not? _____

_____

_____

_____

- -

Name of a piece of artwork your artist created. _____

When did your artist make this piece of artwork? _____

Where is this piece of artwork now? _____

Do you like this piece of artwork? Why or why not? _____

_____

_____

PowerPoint Planning Sheets

For many students as well as teachers, it is helpful to be able to sketch a slide show and design it on paper before designing it on a computer screen. Use the following templates as guides to help you design your presentation.

Slide 1

Slide 2

Slide 3

Slide 4

PowerPoint Planning Sheets *(cont.)*

Slide 1

Slide 2

Slide 3

Slide 4

Slide 5

Slide 6

Slide 7

Slide 8

Slide 9

Glossary

Align—The ability to line up graphic objects along their top or bottom edges.

AutoContent Wizard—A *PowerPoint* tool that generates an outline for you, which you then customize. This is suitable for longer presentations.

AutoLayout—A standard layout menu for art and text locations on a slide. *PowerPoint* provides 21 autolayouts, which you may apply at any time. Some are customized to include space for a graph, table, or organization chart.

Backspace (Windows) - **Delete** (Macintosh)—The keystroke that allows you to delete a selected graphic object.

Cell—This is the place where information is held in a spreadsheet.

Center align—This tab marker sets the tab spacing so that the words are centered on the position where the marker has been placed.

Clip art—A predrawn and preformatted graphic that you can add to a slide.

Combining Slides—You can combine separate slides by opening each one in Outline View, then cutting and pasting them into a single slide.

Continuous Slide Show—A slide show that you have designed to run in a never-ending loop until it is stopped manually. This is particularly suitable for an event such as Open House.

Copy—The command that copies an item onto the Clipboard to be saved for later use elsewhere.

Dialog box—This window appears when a selection has been made. It will ask you questions about how you want the computer to proceed in the activity that has been chosen.

Drawing Toolbar—The toolbar to the immediate left of the slide work area. This is the default drawing toolbar, and contains the selection tool, text tool, and a number of drawing tools.

EDIT...*Undo*—The menu command that lets you cancel the last keystroke you performed.

Exit—The menu command used to leave the *PowerPoint* program.

Grabber handle—The small boxes that appear on the sides and corners of selected graphics. These handles enable you to resize a selected item.

Graph—A *PowerPoint* feature that allows you to type data into a datasheet and then specify the type of graph you want from a wide array of formats.

I-beam—The shape of your cursor when you are typing in a text field.

Glossary *(cont.)*

Justified alignment—This is the alignment marker that arranges the text so that the text is placed in a straight line at both the left and right margins.

Left align—This marker arranges the text to form a straight left margin.

Line Color—A button on the Drawing toolbar that allows you to specify the line color of any selected graphic object in the slide work area.

Menu Bar—The top horizontal bar, above the slide work area, featuring words like **FILE**, **EDIT**, and **VIEW**. These are pulldown menus that allow you to do important tasks like saving and printing your work.

New Slide—A button to the bottom right of the slide work area that lets you create a new slide.

Point size—This is the size of the letters that are typed.

Organization Chart—A feature that lets you create an organization chart and insert it into a *PowerPoint* slide.

Right align—This marker arranges the text to form a straight right margin.

Save—Preserving your presentation in a file format on the hard disk or a floppy disk.

Slide Show—The *PowerPoint* view that plays your finished slide show so you can check the transitions, builds, and timing.

Style—The way that the font is set to look, i.e. bold, italic, underline.

Template—A very important button to the bottom right of the slide work area that lets you choose an overall look or design for your presentation. You can choose templates for black and white overheads, color overheads, or onscreen presentations.

Text tool—An important tool on the Drawing toolbar that allows you to type freeform text onto a *PowerPoint* slide. You can use this to add labels to your slides.

Toolbar—The palette of tools that are available for use.